It's Just a Conversation

What to Say and How to Say It

In
BUSINESS

Debbie Silverman
Trish Carr

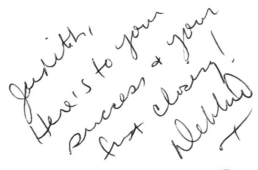

Published by ParkerHouseBooks.com

First Edition: August 2014
Cover design: Candi Parker
Printed in the United States of America

ISBN: 978-0-9895474-5-1

Book Buzz

"Fresh, honest and straightforward – this book gives you everything you need to successfully communicate and get what you want and deserve in business and in life! Model excellence and enjoy this new approach. Trish and Debbie are masters of the spoken word. ~ Yvonne Oswald PhD - Award winning, best-selling author of Every Word has Power

"Everything begins with a conversation and in "It's Just a Conversation," Trish and Debbie have provided the most powerful go-to resource for you to have conversations that deliver desired results for you and those you're in business with. Whether you're having a sales conversation, a discussion with a team member or employee, or just starting one with a new prospect, this book gives you the guidance to create win-win scenarios every time!" ~ Nancy Matthews, Speaker, Author, Business Advisor, Founder of Women's Prosperity Network

"Having a 'win-win' for everyone concerned in any business or personal situation really does start with Just a Conversation! It's Just a Conversation gives you a **huge** *competitive advantage in sales, negotiating, employee relations, networking and more."*
~ Mary A. Molloy, 2X Clarion Award winning author of The Buck Starts Here, and Design Your Own Destiny

"It is not surprising that Trish and Debbie offer wit, wisdom and the WOW factor to everyday business conversations. During my 23 year relationship with Trish, I have watched her impact the lives of so many people, including mine, with her

passion, insight and knowledge about business and life. Now it's your turn!"

    ~ Wendy Watkins, Author, Speaker and Flourishing Strategist

Acknowledgements

As with any book based on real-life experiences, the cast of participants is the foundation of the work. We would like to thank everyone that contributed a conversation and for giving us insight from their experiences so that readers may learn from their failures and successes.

We are eternally grateful to Dr. Yvonne Oswald, Nancy Matthews and Carol Y. Morrgan for their contributions and time editing, guiding us and making our lives so much easier.

Special thanks to you, our reader! By purchasing this book you are advancing the cause for clear and powerful conversations globally.

With love and gratitude we thank Gerri, Bruce, Dan, Nancy and Susan for their relentless support and putting up with our crazy schedule to get this book finished.

Introduction

"Hi Chris, this is Pat, how are you?"

"Hi Pat, I've been better. I'm putting out a fire here at the office."

"OK, I just need a minute of your time. My company just came out with an amazing breakthrough product that would be perfect for you and your company."

"Well it doesn't matter if it's better than oxygen. I'm up to my elbows in work right now. Call me some other time." Click.

Talk about getting started on the wrong foot! Poor Pat didn't have a clue how to steer that conversation in the right direction. And poor Chris, having to deal with a challenge *and* deal with someone pushing a sale. And what did that 30-second conversation do for their relationship? Chris probably thinks Pat didn't really care about Chris' situation. Pat only cared about Pat making a sale. How likely is it that Chris will pick up the phone the next time Pat calls?

When you speak, especially in business, speak as if your life depends on it. Because it does. What you say and how you say it can make the difference between you getting what you want — or not. Your communication is the grease that keeps your business engine going. It's the one skill that makes the greatest difference between success and failure. Whether it's getting a client, forging a partnership, coaching an employee, enrolling team members in your vision or asking for a raise, it all starts with a conversation.

Given that conversations are the lifeblood of our professional life and of life in general, why do some of us spend so little time thinking about what to say and how to say it, while others of us agonize over saying the exact right thing? Why do we often end up in situations we didn't expect

i

because of something we said or didn't say? Why do we spend so much time saying, "Yadda, yadda, yadda...," or "Nothing, nothing, nothing...?" And, what are the hidden messages that we aren't even aware we're giving and getting?

If you're anything like us, chances are you've second guessed yourself after an important conversation. Maybe you asked yourself: *Did I really say that? Did I say everything I wanted to say? Did I make sense? What should I have said next?* Any of these sound familiar? This book moves you from "Hello!" to effectively managing your conversation so you reach a positive outcome. And, when you're feeling challenged or anxious about a particular business conversation, turn to *It's Just a Conversation* as a resource to guide your conversation to a satisfying close.

Investing time learning the different facets of the conversation, like what to say after hello; how to make transitions; and how to end a conversation, will support you in managing your conversations for maximum results in business and in life.

Oh and how could Chris have handled that opening conversation better? Stay tuned...

About this Book

It's Just a Conversation is a resource for you to use   before you open your mouth to speak or before you engage in written conversations, whether those are email, text or other written messages.

In this book we'll show you how to know the next right thing to say, how to avoid miscommunication that can slow down productivity and decrease your bottom line, and how to make the next conversation go as you intended.

It's Just a Conversation guides you through business conversations with real techniques, strategies and tools that we personally use ourselves that we've seen other successful people use, and that we coach others to use. Because of these strategies, we and our clients confidently have conversations that move our businesses and our lives forward. What's more, this book goes beyond oral or written conversations and offers you an understanding of silent conversations – facial expressions, body language, what's not being said and the time between thoughts.

Whether you're a manager, entrepreneur, new in business, an employee wanting to move ahead, or a business student, after reading this book you'll have the tools to make a positive impact in the way you relate to others and the way **THEY RELATE TO YOU!!**

How This Book Is Organized

The chapters are organized so you can read only the topics that interest you, or start at the beginning and go through the whole book. However you choose to take this journey, it's time to start communicating powerfully and confidently.

Sometimes a conversation may go one way and another time the same conversation may take a whole different direction. Throughout each chapter we'll share specific tips on what to say, how to connect with the person you're talking with, and how to develop the conversation to take the relationship to the next level.

> *Good to know tips are centered.*

Table of Contents

Introduction i

About this Book ii

How This Book Is Organized iii

Chapter One

Setting Yourself Up for Success.................................1

It Takes Two to Tango.................................... 1

Emily Post, Where Are You? 2

Conversation Stoppers....................................7

FOCUS, FOCUS, FOCUS 8

Chapter Two

Do You Speak Body?.. 17

Let Me SEE Your Body Talk........................ 17

Creating Rapport.. 23

Body Scan... 27

Gestures.. 33

Chapter Three

Don't Close That Sale! 37

Ditch the Pitch 37

3 Voices in a Conversation.......................... 42

CEObia 45

Nobody Gets in to See the Wizard. Not Nobody.. 50

The Wizard Answered the Phone. Now What?... 56

Get Out of the Cold 59

The Fortune is in the Follow Up 61

Chapter Four

Negotiation 101 73

Setting the Bargaining Table 73

Table Manners.. 77

Play the Game... 82

Win-Win Negotiating.. 87
Chapter Five
Employees and Bosses and Salaries, Oh My 93
    Big Job Interview? 94
    Let's Talk Money... 98
    Get Engaged 103
    You're Fired! 105
Chapter Six
Uneasy Conversations...113
    Communication Breakdowns.............................113
    The Blame Game 119
    'We Need to Talk' (Uh Oh!) 126
    Soft Shoe Conversation..................................130
    Out of Touch? 132
    Asking for the Money 133
Chapter Seven
The New Networking – Creating Relationships Not Just
Leads 141
    Why Network? 142
    Networking Do's & Don'ts 143
    Think Before You Speak................................145
    How Do I Start?..145
    Take it Up a Notch 148
Chapter Eight
Leadership Conversations for the 21st Century 157
    It's an Inside Job...157
    Inspiring for Performance..............................160
    One Size Does NOT Fit All............................166
Just One More Quick Conversation 172
About the Authors...175

Setting Yourself Up for Success

"Think twice before you speak, because your words
and influence will plant the seed of either success or
failure in the mind of another."
~Napoleon Hill, Think & Grow Rich

In This Chapter:
- It Takes Two to Tango
- Emily Post, Where Are You?
- Conversation Stoppers
- FOCUS, FOCUS, FOCUS

It Takes Two to Tango

According to the online edition of the Merriam-Webster Dictionary, a conversation is: "an informal talk involving two people or a small group of people; the act of talking in an informal way."

> *Any number of people can be in a conversation yet only two people can be actively involved at one time talking back and forth.*

Even in today's cyberspace environment with email, chat rooms, tweets, Facebook, LinkedIn, Pinterest, a person can only carry on and be actively involved in a conversation with one other person at a time.

This is the science of conversation. When you operate from this premise, your conversations, in life and in business, are more engaging and rewarding.

Conversations are **interactive** because contributions to a conversation are response reactions to what has previously been said.

Conversations are **spontaneous** because a conversation proceeds, to some extent, unpredictably. However, the scope of that spontaneity may legitimately be limited for the purpose of expediency, for example, a talk show or debate that only has an allotted amount of time.

Emily Post, Where Are You?

Conversations follow **rules of etiquette** because conversations are social interactions that depend on social convention. Not adhering to these rules can devolve and eventually dissolve the conversation.

> **Etiquette** *(e.ti.kɛt), a code of behavior that delineates expectations for social behavior according to contemporary conventional norms within a society, social class or group. ~ Wikipedia*

Conversation etiquette is not new. Emily Post, well-known author and expert on etiquette and manners, wrote about conversational etiquette as early as 1922. Business conversation etiquette differs slightly from social conversation etiquette in that it tends to be more formal, although this is changing with the rise of entrepreneurship and small business ownership -- there's more informality in business than ever before. That said, consider your audience and act accordingly.

Here are a few tips:

Think Before You Speak

Before you speak, stop and think about what you're going to say. Sometimes we speak as we think, rather than formulating our thoughts first. When we speak as we think, the words don't always convey the meaning we intended.

> **Know something about the person or reason that brought you together.**

Most business conversations begin with a common point of interest and then offer the opportunity to gather information about the other person (and their company if applicable). An easy way to learn about the person or persons you're calling or meeting with is to use LinkedIn, Facebook and other Internet resources. Make Google your best friend. You already take it wherever you go so why not ask it questions and make it part of the conversation?

If you're at a business function, networking event or conference, there's usually a common reason for being there. Taking time to prepare yourself with information about the event, the people attending, the industry, etc., helps you better connect with the people you meet.

Adjust Your Formality to Fit the Situation

Being formal is classy. In business, class can take you a long way. Show respect when addressing others and until you're asked to use their first name, use their appropriate title, e.g., Mr., Ms., Dr., etc. Of course, you always want to consider what's appropriate for the situation and act accordingly. If you're at a casual business after hours networking meeting, first name is most likely appropriate.

When being introduced to someone, start with a smile and a firm, friendly handshake. Use their name as they were introduced, either first name or title, e.g., Dan or Mr. Jones. Most importantly, **once you've heard a name, remember it and use it throughout the conversation.**

> *You may want to tap your fingers gently or mentally design a rhyme around the name. Both techniques help you to recall it more easily.*

And while we're on the topic of formality, being formal means using good manners, e.g., no gum chewing, eating or drinking while talking. Watch out for this especially in telephone conversations. Instead, when attending an event with food, stick to small bites and sips and do not eat while on the phone.

By adjusting your formality through each point of the conversation you display a solid balance of confidence and tact.

Stick with Safe Topics

Your words are keys to a successful business conversation. Always keep relationships open and friendly so that your reputation stays immaculate. It can make a difference unexpectedly years down the line.

Be alert to sensitive subjects. In addition to the usual avoidance of politics and religion, when possible, steer clear of personal issue hot buttons.

Need for Reciprocity

An ideal conversation should be a give and take, but too often, it's all "take."

> ### Remember, it's a conversation, not a monologue.

Pay Attention to Signals!

As you chat with others, **be respectful of their time, cut to the chase** and pay close attention to signals that you're losing them. If you continue talking long after they've mentally zoned out, you may find yourself alone, or worse, not invited to the next conversation. The instant you realize you've said too much, take a breath and give someone else a chance to talk. Use humor to lighten it up, "But enough about me," or "Oops, so sorry, I digress…"

When people are no longer engaged, they:

- Yawn

- Stop making eye contact

- Glance around the room (looking for an escape)

- Start backing away

- Stop responding

> *When asked a question, respond for about a minute and then check in to make sure they're with you. Then continue your response as appropriate.*

Equally, give quality answers that connect with them and keep them talking. The goal is to keep a steady flow and keep the person engaged.

Listen, Listen

You have two ears and one mouth for a reason. Use them proportionally. One of the best ways to show you're interested is to listen with your head tilted to one side, nodding. This is an easy way to indicate you're listening and attentive and that in turn, makes it more likely that they'll show interest in you. Give them your undivided attention.

On the telephone, being attentive is vitally important since you can't see the person you're speaking to, which makes it not as easy to gauge their interest level. Let the other person finish their thought without jumping in to finish it for them. When it's your turn to speak, they'll grant you the same courtesy.

> *Use the 4-Second Rule: When the other person stops talking, COUNT to 4 before you speak.*

The "4-Second Rule" makes it more likely the other person finished their thought. You'll ensure you won't be interrupting them, which is an easy way to earn respect.

> *Be mindful of cultural differences.*

You've probably heard the old adage, "When in Rome, do as the Romans do." So be mindful of the differences. For example, someone from Japan may take long pauses between thoughts. In the U.S., people tend to be uncomfortable when no one is speaking and jump right in. When you count to four, not only do you show respect, it gives you an opportunity to consider what was said before responding.

How to show you are listening:

- Maintain eye contact.

- Lean into the conversation, head to one side.

- Nod or interject an occasional, "Yes, I agree" or, "I know what you mean."

- Ask questions (after following the 4-Second Rule).

- *Acknowledge their triumphs with congratulations and empathize with their challenges.*

Conversation Stoppers

Be aware of these common habits that can stop a conversation in its tracks:

- Texting, constantly checking your phone and looking at your watch are all signs that you're not in the moment.

- R-Rated language in a G-Rated situation is not appropriate. (This can be seen as rude and even offensive.)

- Off-color jokes. Keep it clean.

- Interrupting or monopolizing the conversation.

- Randomly changing the conversation to suit yourself.

- Glancing or looking past the person says you are not interested.

- Acting like a know-it-all. (No one knows everything, so don't pretend that you do.)

- Not remembering to introduce people to each other making them feel left out.

- Gossiping. No gossiping about anyone. Ever.

FOCUS, FOCUS, FOCUS

A successful business conversation, or any conversation, is all about FOCUS.

Consider a business conversation where you are totally focused. You remember their name, what they look and sound like, you learn their interests and more importantly, you learn how you can contribute to their success by offering your expertise.

FOCUS is essential to success in everything in life. We'll use FOCUS as an acronym throughout *It's Just a Conversation* to keep you and your conversations in **FOCUS:**

F: FINISH FIRST: Before you have the conversation, set your intention for the outcome you want. Begin with the end in mind and think in reverse.

> *"Prior to a conversation with a high level executive of a major advertising agency, I took the time to think about the outcome I wanted and because I was able to see the end in mind, I crafted the conversation accordingly. As a result, I opened the door to a potentially lucrative relationship."*
> *~Debbie Silverman*

O: OBSERVE the other person and look and listen for ways to establish rapport. It could be simply noticing something they're wearing, e.g., company logo on a pin, hat, tee shirt, etc. It could be their posture, gestures, and/or facial expressions. It could be the language they use, their accent or their words. The object is to identify commonalities so you establish rapport and create a great first impression.

Mary Molloy, two-time Clarion Award winning author of *The Buck Starts Here* and *Design Your Own Destiny*, shares this insightful story of how a simple comment can lead to an affluent contact and a meaningful connection:

> *"I was wearing this kelly green jacket and a guy came up to me and introduced himself, 'Hi, I'm Kevin Harrington.' I said, 'Hi, I'm Mary Molloy.' 'Mary Molloy,' he said, 'what a great Irish name and you're wearing green and green is*

my favorite color.' I told him, 'Well, I'm wearing green and the name is Molloy, but I'm actually Sicilian.' He was obviously surprised and asked, 'You're Sicilian? With your coloring?'''

Mary gave Kevin a light-hearted lesson on Sicily's history explaining that because it's in the middle of the Mediterranean, anyone wanting to conquer Europe came through Sicily. Hannibal and the Spaniards were dark, the Vikings were blonde, half the island has light coloring and the other has dark. Mary continues:

"'Wow! That's really fantastic,' he said. And then we started getting into a bigger conversation. We started talking about other things, where we live, and about flying in and out of different airports. So, we get into this great conversation and do you know who Kevin Harrington is? Do you know the products 'As Seen on TV'? That's Kevin. He owns that billion dollar company and he knows who I am. I connected with him with just a conversation, 'Mary Molloy, what a great Irish name,' and the next thing you know, I'm connected with Kevin Harrington."

Kevin's observation of Mary's jacket made for a memorable introduction that opened a long term relationship that led to Mary and Kevin doing business together today.

C: CLARIFY IMPORTANT POINTS by asking questions. Clarifying questions confirm that the message, intent and emotions you observed were what the speaker meant to convey.

Also, if you didn't hear the person, it's a good way to get them to reiterate their point.

Don't say: *"What?"*

Do say: *"I missed your last comment, would you please repeat it?"*

When clarifying information, paraphrase, don't parrot. Repeating the speaker's exact words can sound patronizing. Instead, rephrase the statement using your own words.

For example, suppose a business associate, Sam, comes to you and says, "I just had a conversation with John and he's excited about the new project."

Don't say: *"So, Sam, what I heard is that you just had a conversation with John and he's excited about the new project?"* saying it almost verbatim.

Do say: *"Sam, I'm happy to hear he's excited about the project. Tell me more..."*

U: YOU ARE UNIQUE: Be true to yourself. BE AUTHENTIC. Some people think when you're first meeting someone that you need to be super-professional. In our experience, most people like *real* conversations that don't force them to act like people they aren't. When you see an opportunity to bring humor or to personalize a conversation, take it – and do it — *with the caveat of keeping it tasteful and professional.* Being real, being funny and being human opens barriers immediately and that shift allows for a better conversation.

Mary Molloy's green jacket story illustrates what can happen when you take every opportunity to be your unique self and talk about personal things as well as business.

11

S: STAY IN THE MOMENT:

"Stay in the moment means you show up and stay laser focused in the here and now...you stay fully present... physically, emotionally and mentally. In this state you are alert, observant and open to what your team members have to offer," says Mary T. Curtis, international speaker, trainer, coach and graduate of the world-renowned Second City Conservatory program.

> **Stay in the moment without creating mental scripts of what you'll say next.**

When you stay in the moment you give yourself a chance to hear what's really being said and then you're better prepared to share your point of view.

Staying in the 'now' isn't always easy. There's so much going on in our minds!

"As humans we are prone to judgment, assumptions, emotions and personal agendas...all of which take us out of the moment," says Mary T. Curtis.

People often pre-script while waiting their turn to talk. This is especially obvious when people are asked to introduce themselves at a meeting. We can get so caught up on our own story and introduction that we often don't catch golden nuggets of information about our colleagues.

For the best flow, a conversation needs spontaneity. When people are in the moment, their phrases have the feeling of freshness and authenticity, even though they may not be well-crafted or even grammatically correct.

Here's an example of **NOT** staying in the moment and the negative outcome that ensued:

12

"I remember introducing myself at a business networking event and I was the last to speak with 35 people in the room. I was so focused on how I was going to introduce myself, you know, the 30-second elevator speech — my title and expertise — that I totally lost sight of the experience and names of the 34 women that came before me. I also noticed that the one or two women that really stayed in the moment and listened to what was being said were the ones that other women wanted to spend time with and ultimately do business with. That was a powerful lesson. Since then I give my best effort to staying focused and in the moment and as a result, I'm connecting more quickly to more people."
~Debbie Silverman

"All of life takes place in the moment. What is happening in the moment is your key to possibility. And if you miss the moment...you miss the possibility!"
Mary T. Curtis

Here's a simple exercise to stay in the moment. Think of a person, place or thing. Really focus on that particular thought. Now let your mind wander to another person, place or thing. When you feel your mind shifting to another thought, say to yourself, 'stay in the moment' and take your mind back to the original thought. It takes some practice. You will notice in a short time that you are more focused and more in the moment.

Decide on your goal, then stay in the moment without judgment; manage your emotions and let go of outcomes. This will automatically lead to more successful business relationships.

Setting Yourself Up for Success Worksheet

Here's a worksheet to plan your next business conversation. As you plan, remember to **FOCUS**:

F: FINISH FIRST: What is the one outcome you want to achieve?

_____

_____

_____

O: OBSERVE: You can observe something about the person you are about to converse with by doing some detective work online. Check out the person, company and industry on Google, LinkedIn, Facebook, and other sources.

Write 3 things you observed or discovered about that person/company to use in a conversation:

1. _____
2. _____
3. _____

C: CLARIFY: Prepare 3 possible questions for your conversation:

1. _____
2. _____
3. _____

U: UNIQUE: Being unique is a mindset. Stay true to yourself.

S: STAY IN THE MOMENT: You can practice staying in the moment before you get to the conversation. Think of a person, place or thing. Really focus on that particular thought. Now let your mind wander to another person, place or thing. When you feel your mind shifting to another thought, say to yourself, 'stay in the moment' and take your mind back to the original thought.

If you find yourself shuffling from one topic to the next say this, STAY IN THE MOMENT! Practice this on a daily basis and you will see that you will have an outstanding amount of focus.

Download a copy of this worksheet at:
http://ItsJustaConversationBook.com/downloads

Do You Speak Body?

"I speak two languages - Body and English."
~ Mae West, American actress, singer, playwright,
screenwriter and sex symbol

In This Chapter:
- Let Me SEE Your Body Talk
- Creating Rapport
- Body Scan
- Gestures

Let Me SEE Your Body Talk

You may remember the Olivia Newton-John song "Physical" that sings, *"Let me hear your body talk."* Your body does actually talk, except we should be singing, *"Let me SEE your body talk."* Your body language speaks volumes. This crucial conversation, *the silent conversation,* can make the biggest difference in our success – and is one most people aren't even aware of.

Did you know that experts say only a small percentage of communication involves actual words? Only 7%, to be exact. In his study, *Decoding of Inconsistent Communications,* Dr. Albert Mehrabian found that 55% of communication is visual *(body language, eye contact)* and 38% is vocal *(pitch, speed, volume, tone of voice).*

You've probably heard the expression, *"You never get a second chance to make a good first impression."* Did you know that many experts say that the first impression is made in the first **seven seconds** of a conversation? And, get this — what happens in those seven seconds often has little to do with what we say and instead is about what we *convey in our physical appearance and body language.*

An expert in the fast developing field of Human Behavioral Technology and award winning, best-selling author of *Every Word Has Power,* Yvonne Oswald, PhD, says that it may be even less than seven seconds:

> *"This goes way back into the past, over 200,000 years, and is deep wired into your neurology as the flight or fight response. You actually have 0.012 of a second to know if someone is a friend or not!*
>
> *The first thing to understand about body language is that we as human beings all need to be in the same 'club'. We set up clubs and if we recognize that someone is in our club, we're more inclined to like them better. So if you're not in our club; that is, if you look different or you act differently than others, people tend to be a little suspicious of you until you prove yourself."*

Consider that every time you meet someone the first time, you naturally make a decision as to whether they're in your club. And so does everyone who meets you. Don't think so? Dr. Yvonne shared this story to make the point:

> *"When I first started out in business, I went to a woman's executive networking meeting. It was summer so I put on a really nice pink skirt-suit, some cute white shoes and a white handbag and I thought I looked really smart. As I walked into the breakfast meeting, every single woman in there, and there must have been 250 women, was dressed in dark blue and black. And, they were all in business pant-suits.*
>
> *My heart sank. But I had already paid my $60 and decided to stay. Shortly after I sat down, some people did approach me and I realized really quickly they either completely ignored me because I was wearing different colors and had a whole different energy than them, or they came up to me and were interested **because** I looked different.*
>
> *There were two very different responses."*

People will be drawn to you because you're in their club or because you're not. So what should you do in a business situation? Dr. Oswald goes on to say,

> *"So you'll get that kind of different response from your body language, the clothes you're wearing, your hairstyle, or even the makeup you wear. People will recognize it and immediately draw you in or not be sure about you and not want to engage. That first impression counts so much. When you're going to a business meeting it's useful to find out ahead of time about the kind of people who are going there and match them accordingly."*

We're with Dr. Oswald. Why take a chance and wear a pink suit and run the risk of alienating anyone? Stick with being in the *right* club when it comes to making a good first impression.

Here's another body language tip from Dr. Oswald that will help you make that great first impression:

> *"An instant friend maker is the 'eyebrow flick.' When saying hello, just quickly raise your eyebrows, open your eyes wide and show as many teeth as you can as you greet them. The eyebrow flick opens your eyes, dilates your pupils, and the person on the other end gets an instant flood of feel-good endorphins."*

Since we have only seconds to make a first impression, how should we prepare? To get your body and facial expressions to clearly communicate what you want to say, you must remember to **FOCUS:**

F: FINISH FIRST: Think about how you want to be remembered after the conversation – think in reverse. Your body language and facial expressions say volumes about you before you ever open your mouth.

> *Whether someone can see you or not, your body language and facial expressions control your feelings which control how you communicate with others.*

This is also true on the phone, and in other remote forms of communication like email and text.

For example, if you call someone while feeling tension in your face and neck you may come across as angry, frustrated or as lacking confidence and control. If, however, you have a smile on your face, even if you have to put it on and it's not genuine, it changes your demeanor, changes your energy and it affects the outcome. A smile puts the tone in your voice that you are friendly and approachable.

> ***Practice facial expressions and body language in the mirror.***

Pay attention to your posture, notice how you stand. Are you standing or sitting erect? Standing erect with shoulders back, chest out and head held high conveys POWER, STATUS and CONFIDENCE.

> ***Great posture makes it easier to express yourself from your heart, rather than your head. When thoughts and words come from your heart, they are believable.***

- A slouched posture is often associated with a lack of confidence and/or a lack of engagement or interest.

- Are your feet close together or confidently apart?
  If your feet are too close together you may give the impression of being shaky and unsure of what you are saying.

- Widen your stance to look solid and confident.

> *Relax your knees and center your weight in your lower body to give you stability.*

Sit in a chair and notice how you're sitting. Are you sitting tall or are you slouching?

What's amazing about practicing in the mirror is that you can actually feel how you change your mood by adjusting your body and face. With this understanding and FOCUS, you can immediately make changes to be a more successful you.

> *Be careful of saying one thing while your body language conveys the opposite. For instance saying, "I love your hair!" while shaking your head. Focus on body language and facial expressions that project a confident and successful YOU.*

O: OBSERVE AND MAKE CHANGES: Model people who are better than you are at sales, negotiating, networking and other business conversations. Study how they stand, sit, how they use their hands, their facial expressions, where their feet are placed, and if they lean into the conversation or sit back.

C: CLARIFY: Be clear on what you want to communicate and make sure your body gets the memo.

U: USE BODY LANGUAGE to your advantage. Be aware of what you're reflecting with your body language because you may not always convey what you really feel. For example, keeping your hands in your pockets, stiffly by your side, or folded in front "like a fig leaf" can give the impression that you're insecure – whether you are or not. Crossing your arms may be interpreted that you're closed off even though that may not be your intention. Understand what may be perceived about you and use body language to your advantage.

S: STAY IN THE MOMENT: Stop thinking about what you're going to say next. Rather, pay attention to and consciously consider what your body language and facial expressions are saying for you.

> *Remember that the body language and facial expressions in your culture or country may not be the same around the world.*

The most universal symbol is a SMILE. It creates positive, creative energy. A smile is contagious.
Remember yours!

> *Smile. A smile speaks volumes, even on the phone.*

Creating Rapport

Rapport is the connection between two people; the spoken and unspoken words and body language that say we're on the same page. *"Rapport increases your sense of self-confidence and charisma and you can immediately make a great first impression,"* says Dr. Oswald.

Rapport is the first round of acceptance into their club.

> ***Rapport is absolutely necessary for any successful business conversation. Without rapport, sales don't happen, negotiations don't work, job interviews don't succeed and businesses stop thriving.***

A technique that easily creates rapport is matching and mirroring one's style of behavior and body language — *"although it needs to be subtle so that the other person doesn't notice what you're doing or thinks you're making fun of them,"* states Dr. Oswald.

Mirroring someone's movements is like looking into a mirror. If he or she moves their left hand to their face, you move your right hand to your face. Matching and mirroring is not just a good idea that someone came up with – it has its roots in biology and survival. Dr. Oswald explains:

> *"When you meet someone, your mirror neurons are stimulated and there are only a few species on earth that have mirror neurons; humans have them, dolphins, elephants, parrots and monkeys have them. Mirror neurons are very special because they enable us to have empathy and understanding so that we can survive together as a group species.*
>
> *Thousands of years ago, our ancestors learned to survive as a group and in order to be accepted as part of*

the tribe you had to match and mirror the other person's body language. Now, that means that if someone has their hands by their side when they're speaking to you, your hands should be by your side; if you're sitting down and one person crosses their legs, your job is to cross your legs as well.

When you do this, you'll find the rapport building is amazingly efficient, you don't need to work at getting to know them very much; they'll just feel like they've known you forever."

The Mirror and Match technique quickly builds rapport. If a conversation is not going the way you want it to, this is the first place to look. It's possible you're not matching and mirroring. Dr. Oswald shared this perfect example of how matching and mirroring can make things go smoothly:

"I was at a TV audition with my young daughter, Katie, and while she was being interviewed, the owner of the agency kept interfering. She was quite brusque and kept interrupting. It didn't make us feel very good. I looked at the interviewer, Katie and myself and noticed we all had the same body language. We were sitting forward with our arms on our knees, nodding, smiling, and it was like, wow, this is so cool, we're passing this audition.

It suddenly occurred to me that the woman who was the boss and decision maker, was sitting back in her chair with a phone in her hand looking down, and I thought, 'Uh-oh, we're not including her in our club – that's why she's interfering so much.

I sat up in the chair, put my hand to my chin as though I was holding a phone and leaned back. The owner immediately said, 'Oh, yes marvelous. She's in, she'll do.'"

This stuff really works! Add matching and mirroring to your conversation toolkit and watch your results skyrocket.

When you match and mirror, pay attention to and "match" the other person's:

- Tone of voice. Pay attention to the speed, volume and energy in their voice.

- Words and phrases they use and add these to your conversation.

- Posture and gestures. Subtly match their posture and gestures.

- Way of handling information. Do they give lots of detail or do they talk about the big picture? Give them information the same way they give it to you.

> *DO NOT match and mirror when someone is angry or frustrated unless you want to escalate that feeling. In a situation where negative emotions are high, express concern, with your head tilted to one side, rather than match and mirror.*

Body Scan

A body scan takes only seconds and gives you insight into the message the other person is sending. Understanding body language provides an edge in conversation and connecting. Understand though, that these are generalities. Keep in mind the situation and the circumstance. Crossing your arms may mean you're closed off OR it may mean the room is cold. Some things to consider:

Body Angle

First, look at the person's body angle (seated or standing). Jan Hargrave in her book, *Strictly Business, Body Language,*[1] lists the following body behaviors and the message each conveys:

- Slumped posture = low spirits, dejection.

- Erect posture = high spirits, energy and confidence.

- Leaning forward = interest, openness, positive attitude toward other person.

- Leaning away = distrusting, defensive and disinterested.

- Sitting on edge of chair = receptive, ready to listen.

Here's an example of how body language when taken to the extreme had a negative effect.

----

[1] *Parts excerpted from Jan Hargrave's, Strictly Business, Body Language.*

27

"*Early in my career, I worked for a large advertising agency in New York. My boss at the time was a short woman (about 4'11") and I am nearly 6 feet tall. One day, to make a point she actually stood on her desk so that she could talk down to me. When we walked to meetings, she made me walk either behind her or several feet in front of her so that I wouldn't intimidate her. This was my first exposure to the business world. I had the utmost respect for her until she pulled these crazy 'power' tactics. She made me realize that bosses are human like the rest of us and have a lot of insecurities too.*"
~Debbie Silverman

Face and Eyes

Next, look at the face and eyes. It's been said that the face and eyes are the windows to the soul. Let's start with the eyes. When you speak with someone, make and maintain eye contact.

> **Successful business people make and maintain eye contact 50-60% of the time.**

What are the eyes saying?

- Too little eye contact could mean the person is not paying attention, is covering up their true emotions, is being insincere or is being impolite.

- A glazed look or looking around the room could mean boredom.

- Direct eye contact signals honesty and interest.

- People who don't do eye contact well are typically considered to be hiding something.

- A natural way to maintain eye contact is to look away occasionally for a couple of seconds as you listen then return to eye contact.

> ***Maintain eye contact long enough to notice what color they are.***

What is the face saying?

Facial expressions and your eyes tell a story that other body parts may be hiding. A person's health can also affect their facial expression:

- Anxiety causes a person's face to show stress.

- A quick flush or redness in someone's face may indicate that something is not right.

- Depressed people smile wider and longer to cover up that they are unhappy.

Arms and Hands

You may see people with their arms folded across their chest. There are different variations of this gesture. In most cases it can symbolize a body block or an attempt to close down or guard themselves from an unfavorable situation.

For example, if a person's arms are crossed and you can't see their hands, it could mean that there is distrust or a negative attitude. (Interestingly this is a universal gesture of avoidance.)

When arms are crossed and fingers of one hand are visible, it's generally a positive gesture that means the person is open and listening.

> *If you're in a negotiation and you see the other person cross their arms without showing one hand, hand them something to break the barrier.*

Do not mirror negative body language–match it!

If they have their arms crossed you might cross your hands then smile at them and open your hands. Unconsciously they will mirror you and open up.

Some things to know about hands:

- Open and relaxed hands can be a positive selling signal.

- Tightly clinched fists could mean defensiveness.

- Self-touching gestures such as the hand on the chin, ear, nose, hair might indicate tension or nervousness.

- Hands and fingers that fidget (with hair, pens, paper clips, etc.) can be seen as annoying and typically mean the person is impatient or nervous.

- Hands and palms facing down is a movement known as the 'Leveler' and denotes confidence and authority. It's as though you are smoothing out a tablecloth as you speak.

And while we're at it, let's talk about the all-important handshake.

> *"I remember meeting a man who wanted to be a speaker at Women's Prosperity Network's international conference. When he introduced himself he grabbed my fingers in a classic 'dead fish' handshake. I stopped him and said, 'Wait a minute, let's get a good handshake here,' and I showed him what a firm, confident handshake felt like. He smiled and said he didn't realize he was supposed to shake a woman's hand like he would a man's. The fact that he took my hand in a wimpy shake could have made the difference between him being on our stage or not. Your handshake adds to your first impression — no floppy fish or strongman grips."*
> *~Trish Carr*

Carol Kinsey Goman, PhD, body language coach and *Forbes* magazine contributor says, *"While a great handshake is important for all professionals, it is especially key for women – whose confidence is evaluated by the quality of their handshake even more than it is with their male counterparts."*

Many men THINK they're supposed to offer a fish hand to women and many women don't realize that to display confidence they should shake hands with men as equals. Always give a firm handshake that displays confidence and warmth.

Legs and Feet

Keep your legs uncrossed in a negotiation or a selling situation.

According to a study of 2,000 people by Nierenberg and Calero in *How to Read a Person Like a Book*, no sales occurred while the participants had their legs crossed. Crossed legs or crossed ankles signal that the mind is not completely open.

> ***If you do have to cross your legs, cross them in the same direction as the person with whom you are conversing.***

> *"A client of mine, who appears on QVC, was presenting her product along with a specialist she brought in to help her sell the product. Both were seated in high rise chairs next to each other. The specialist crossed her legs away from my client and my client crossed her legs away from the specialist. At that point it looked like they didn't really know or like each other and their energy was not as intense."*
> ~Debbie Silverman

> ***To make the sale or win at the negotiation table, keep both feet planted on the floor. Uncrossed legs send a message of cooperation, confidence and friendly interest in the other person.***

Gestures

Gestures can reveal a lot about what someone is really thinking and identify the deeper meaning that the speaker does not or cannot articulate.

Key gestures to recognize in any sales and negotiation scenario:

- The mouth cover may mean protection from letting the wrong words slip out.

- If the person is *not* speaking and touches the side of their nose or covers their mouth, it can be an indication that they feel that the speaker is being dishonest.

- The chin rest combined with an index finger point can convey genuine interest and evaluation.

- The eye or ear rub can mean you don't really see what I'm telling you or hear what I'm telling you because I'm lying to you.

Remember to do a quick body scan on yourself before you engage in conversation. Just as you notice things about others, they notice things about you.

Do You Speak Body? Worksheet

Remember, the silent conversation, or body language, has a greater impact than the words we say or tone of voice we use.

Before you speak, **FOCUS:**

F: FINISH FIRST: What is the outcome you want to achieve?

Determine the message you want to convey and check your body language and facial expressions in the mirror. Practice with a friend or associate to make sure you are communicating your intended message.

_____

_____

_____

_____

O: OBSERVE: Study successful people in your line of work. See how they handle themselves, how they gesture, their facial expressions, etc.

Write down three things you like about their facial expressions and body language:

1. _____

2. _____

3. _____

Identify at least two gestures that you want to change and make that change now. Ask a friend to keep you aware by pointing out every time you make that gesture so that you can change it:

Gesture #1_____

Gesture #2_____

C: **CLARIFY:** *Clarify* in your mind what you want to communicate and make sure your body gets the memo.

U: **USE MATCHING AND MIRRORING** to create rapport and an understanding. Practice matching and mirroring with a friend before the real conversation.

S: **STAY IN THE MOMENT:** Practice staying in the moment and making eye contact comfortably and without staring.

Download a copy of this worksheet at:
http://ItsJustaConversationBook.com/downloads

It's Just a Conversation

Don't Close That Sale!

*"It's not about closing the sale,
it's about opening the relationship."*
~ Trish Carr

In This Chapter:
- Ditch the Pitch
- 3 Voices In a Conversation
- CEObia
- Nobody Gets in to See the Wizard. Not Nobody
- The Wizard Answered the Phone, Now What?
- Get Out of the Cold
- The Fortune is in the Follow Up

Ditch the Pitch

How do you craft a winning sales conversation? Ditch the Pitch. "Pitch" describes what sales people used to do — throw as much information as possible at prospects hoping to sell a product or service before the buyer could hang up the phone or slam the door.

In today's world, when you use the word "pitch" people assume there's a catch and look for something to object to.

> *Instead of a "pitch," make a recommendation. Base your recommendation on specific knowledge you have about your prospect. A "recommendation" lets prospects know you want to engage in a conversation that will improve some aspect of their business or their life, not just sell something.*

Plan your sales call in advance And be sure to **FOCUS:**

F: FINISH FIRST: Plan your sales call starting with the end in mind. Identify your objectives and set your intention. Say to yourself, *"At the end of this call they will agree to meet with me."* Or, *"At the end of this sales call they will buy from me."*

> *Think big and don't be afraid to ask largely. We're going to repeat this one –THINK BIG AND DON'T BE AFRAID TO ASK LARGELY.*

"At a sales conference I was given an opportunity to ask a 7-figure business coach for anything I wanted to help my business. I asked for four of his best leads. He said four

was too much and asked if one would do. I always start high. Had I asked for only one, I may not have gotten any."
    ~Debbie Silverman

O: OBSERVE AND LISTEN to what's being said and written about the person (and their company if applicable). Check out LinkedIn, Google, other Social Media, trade newspapers, and company websites for more information about the person, company and industry. The more you know about them, the more relatable you can be. The more you show interest in them, the more you build affinity in any relationship.

C: CLARIFY*:* Remember to clarify what's said by asking questions. Asking questions helps you understand what the situation or challenge is and focuses your attention on the person with whom you are speaking, rather than on yourself.

U: YOU ARE UNIQUE: Be true to yourself, *BE AUTHENTIC.*

S: STAY IN THE MOMENT: When you stay in the moment and follow these FOCUS tips, you'll have a productive sales conversation. Listen, remain in the moment, uncover clues, ditch the pitch and create a relationship.

Successful Salespeople Know...

1.   A lot about their buyer. Did you know that the average buyer spends about 70% of their time researching you or your company before they buy? How much time do you spend researching your buyer?

2. To talk 20% of the time and listen the other 80%. Let your client or prospect talk most of the time and when you talk, tell them how you can improve their situation or make something easier for them.

> ***Don't elaborate on the functions of your product and sell them on the features or characteristics. Instead, share the benefits or the value of the service or product. It's not about what a product or service does, it's what that product or service does for them that matters.***

For example:

Don't Say: *"This pan has a Teflon coating and a 12" surface."*

Do Say: *"The Teflon pan makes sure that no food sticks making cleanup a breeze and the large 12" heating surface allows for one-pan cooking - perfect for a big family like yours."*

3. How to match and mirror, e.g., use your prospect's words and similar tonality and/or body language, to create a connection.

4. How to connect the value of their solution to that specific buyer -- if not, the buyer may not give you the time of day.

For example:

"Ms. Richman, this technology will eliminate the issue you said you're having managing four different databases."

5.   To tell their prospect how their product or service can cut costs, reduce time, increase profits. Give specific examples and quantify wherever possible. Numbers and percentages offer perspective, make it easy to visualize the value and make it tangible.

For example:

"Mr. Garcia, because this machine uses the newest technology, it reduces electricity 25%. Add that cost savings to the ability to increase production and you increase your bottom line by $10K a month."

6. How to ask for a commitment at the end of the conversation, and **Ask Largely**.

> **When you go in with the idea that you're going to have a conversation and build a relationship, you'll have a much better success rate. Remember, it's not about you — it's about them!**

"Pretend that every single person you meet has a sign around his or her neck that says, Make Me Feel Important. Not only will you succeed in sales, you will succeed in life."
  ~*Mary Kay Ash, Founder, Mary Kay Cosmetics*

> *Want to make great presentations every time? Go to http://TrishCarr.com and get your FREE copy of "The 3 P's of Powerful Presentations," the proven formula for getting it right every time.*

> **Your first goal is to get the prospect's attention and agreement to have an engaged conversation about how you can serve them and/or solve a specific problem or need.**

3 Voices in a Conversation

There are three voices in any conversation – or *"three conversations occurring at the same time,"* says Joe Matthews, *Entrepreneur Magazine* contributor. In his article, *This Is What the Ultimate Sales Conversation Sounds Like,* Joe says in any sales situation, there are these three conversations:

1. The conversation between the buyer and the salesperson.

2. The conversation the buyer is having with themselves.

3. The conversation the salesperson is having with themselves.

If you think you don't talk to yourself, think again. Sometimes we listen and respond to the little voice in our heads instead of paying attention to the other person.

For example, a typical sales conversation may go something like this:

Salesperson: *"I wanted to follow-up on the proposal we submitted and answer any questions or concerns you may have."*

Buyer (what they're thinking): *"Their proposal didn't address my needs and I'm leaning towards another company. Should I share my real concerns or just tell her everything is fine? I'm really not in the mood for another sales pitch right now."*

Buyer (what they say): *"I don't have any questions. Everything looks fine. I have a call right now and need to jump off."*

Salesperson (what they're thinking): *"Sounds like something is a bit off. Should I probe more and see what is going on?"*

Salesperson (what they say): *"Great to hear! I look forward to hearing your decision when you're ready."*

> *All buying decisions occur in conversation #2 – the conversation the buyer has with themselves, in their head.*

The average salesperson spends too much time:

- Engaging the buyer in surface-level information in conversation #1, between the buyer and salesperson.

- Plotting what they'll say next, keeping them in conversation #3, the one they have with themselves.

- Ignoring their instincts and accepting conversation #1, between the buyer and salesperson, as the way it really is, rather than exploring what the buyer is really thinking.

> *Be best in class. Best-in-class salespeople know how to bring conversation #2, the buyer's conversation with themselves, out in the open. This enables the buyer and the seller to have an open and honest dialogue about what's really going on and gives the buyer freedom to voice their concerns and engage in a win-win negotiation or problem solving opportunity.*

To bring the conversation the buyer is having with themselves out in the open and to get the buyer to want to share what they are feeling or experiencing, the salesperson must first create **trust and credibility.**

Here are a few questions to gain access to the buyer's conversation with themselves:

- When you said (whatever it is they said), what did you mean by that?

- I hear some hesitation. What made you pause?

- Since my goal is to understand how I can best serve your needs, what didn't I ask that I should have?

- I feel like there's a conversation that we should be having that we aren't. What aren't we talking about that we should be?

When you learn how to get to what your buyer is really thinking and feeling, you increase your results exponentially.

> *One of the best ways to be a better salesperson is to listen for what the buyer isn't telling you and then bring it out in the open.*

CEObia

CEObia, is that even a word? It is now.

According to us, CEObia is the fear of speaking to a "C" level executive (CEO, COO, CMO, CFO), or to anyone with a lot of letters after their name, or anyone that causes you to feel a little anxious or intimidated.

Why is there trepidation about talking to these people? After all, they drink their coffee the same way we do, right? Why is there uneasiness around people with a "C" in their title?

Speaking with peers is relatively easy. The stakes aren't as high. If you mess up and say the incorrect thing, they'll usually let it pass.

But executives can be different. Time with high level people is precious and you want to make every moment count. One misstep may head you out the door.

> "Corporate decision makers are extremely protective of their time. Because they're under constant pressure to deliver results, they guard their schedule from interruptions of any sort. That's why they don't answer the phone or return phone calls – even though they know it's rude." says Author, Jill Konrath in her book, *Selling To Big Companies*.

What can you do to prepare to talk to a "C" level person? Remember to **FOCUS:**

F: FINISH FIRST: Consider what you want the outcome to be, think in reverse. Set your intention.

O: OBSERVE: To build rapport, pay attention and listen to what the executive is willing to share with you; if in person, observe their office and pictures (family, pets, activity, etc.). Ask what is important to them about their company needs right now. Repeat their response verbatim and they will then want to hear more about your product/service.

Human Behavioral Technologist, Dr. Yvonne Oswald offers this insight:

> "Listen to the words they use and repeat them back so that they get that you understand them. If they use words such as see and look, they are primarily visual. If they use words such as listen, and hear, they are auditory. If they use words such as feel or touch base, they are kinesthetic. If they use phrases such as, comes to mind, explain, or understand, they

are digital communicators. By simply repeating their same words back in your own sentences, you establish rapport and understanding on a deeper level."

C: CLARIFY: Be sure to clarify points and remember to make it about the executive and not about you or your company. When they ask you about your company, that's your cue to **show** them how you can do something to make a difference for them.

U: UNIQUE: You are unique, be yourself.

S: STAY IN THE MOMENT: When you find yourself in your head instead of focused on your prospect, catch yourself and stay in the moment. With a little practice, staying present becomes second nature.

> *Creating TRUST is one of the most important things you can do to build relationships. Keep your word, do what you said you'd do, go over and above.*

Trust starts with rapport and continues when you keep your promises. Jann Sabin, President of the award winning creative ad agency, Brandbooster, shares this example of how trust builds confidence and repeat business:

"In the course of doing internal research for a client, we interviewed a high-level executive at the company. Shortly after the interview, he was regretting some of the things he said. I gave him my word that his name would not be

connected with the specific information reported and I promised to leave out certain things that were mentioned."

"About a year later I received another phone call from this person, but now he was at the parent company of the one that was my client. He was in charge of a big initiative and invited me to come to talk about it. He told me that he was very doubtful that time a year ago when I promised him anonymity, especially because my relationship with the Director of Marketing on the former project spanned many years. Because of the trust I developed, I went on to work with this parent company for over six years."

Promises kept are never forgotten. Trust is an immensely valuable asset. Let's face it, even with these great tips you still may get nervous. That's OK. A little nervousness keeps you on your game. The trick is to manage your mind so you stay in control, remain optimistic and expect the best. Manage your mind by watching your language to yourself. Don't call it "nervous." You're actually feeling the same adrenaline coursing through your body when you're "nervous" as when you're "excited." Why not call it excited and program your mind for a positive experience?

Here's a simple technique to use before you meet with someone or call them on the phone that will take away any "nervous" feeling. This is a terrific technique for anything in life that makes you feel uncomfortable. It's a way to confuse the mind so that you won't get nervous about a particular situation. Use this NLP[2] technique to quickly shift how you feel and to free your mind to be creative.

---

[2] *NLP, or Neuro Linguistic Programming, is a technique used to reprogram your subconscious to give you what you want. It's an effective way to change behavior quickly.*

48

Ask yourself these questions, inserting the name or title of the person you're meeting:

- What would happen if I could speak with _____?

- What wouldn't happen if I could speak with _____?

- What would happen if I couldn't speak with _____?

- What wouldn't happen if I couldn't speak with _____?

Continue asking yourself these questions until you feel confused. It's OK if you can't answer them all - that's the point. When you reach the point of confusion you'll smile and say, *"I can't remember what I was concerned about!"*

When talking with high level decision makers, improve your chances of success by remembering to:

- Focus on their business.

- Be explicit in the difference you make.

- Personalize every contact.

- Be confident in your product, your service and yourself.

- Speak honestly.

- Master the 30-second response.

- Show them how others do things. (They're especially interested in how similar companies have tackled the very same challenges they are facing.)

- Talk with them as peers.

> *"Nobody gets in to see the wizard. Not nobody."*
> *~L. Frank Baum, The Wonderful Wizard of Oz*

Nobody Gets in to See the Wizard. Not Nobody.

When attempting to reach a decision maker, have you ever felt like Dorothy, the Tin Man, the Scarecrow and the Lion trying to get in to see the Wizard? It's not easy – and the guard makes you prove your worthiness to see the Great and Powerful Oz.

Business is very much like Oz in that way. The gatekeeper is there to protect executive level management. This gatekeeper, whose title might be executive assistant, administrative aide, executive secretary, or even receptionist, is a highly trusted partner to the person you want to meet.

Gatekeepers are fountains of knowledge. They're intimately aware of the company's goals, objectives, key business initiatives and priorities. They can be a valuable asset.

When you create a relationship with the gatekeeper you have an ***ally*** who wants to introduce you to their boss.

> ***Treat gatekeepers with as much respect***
> ***as you would decision makers.***

- Treat gatekeepers as respected colleagues. Help them understand why they and their boss will benefit from speaking with you. Be sure you include what's in it for the gatekeeper too!

- Be prepared for common questions, "What is this regarding?" and have a great response ready.

- Gatekeepers are an invaluable inside source. To learn more about their company and their boss, develop positive relationships with them.

As with any business conversation, it's imperative to prepare for the gatekeeper conversation as well. FOCUS and know that your goal is to go well beyond just getting through. Your goal is to create an <u>ally</u>.

In her book, *Selling to Big Companies*, Jill Konrath contends:

> "If you believe that what you sell truly makes a difference to an organization, then you are already aligned with the gatekeeper's objective. Your challenge then is simply to help the gatekeeper understand why you need to talk to or meet with their boss. Their antennas are up at all times and are acutely tuned in to the language of a salesperson. If you slip into that mode even a little bit, they'll block you from getting in."

When gatekeepers screen calls they want to know:

1. Who you are

2. Why you are calling

3. If the decision maker is expecting to hear from you

> *You may bend the formality rule if you reach a CEO's gatekeeper and you know the CEO's first name. Using their first name may give you a better chance of being connected.*

A typical conversation may go something like this:

Gatekeeper: Mr. Johnson's office, may I help you?

Seller: This is Pat Smith from XYZ Consulting. I'd like to speak with Jack please.

Gatekeeper: What is this regarding? (Always be prepared with your response. You already have this ready – your response is the same as if you had reached the decision maker.)

> *This very brief answer should include a referral, mention of working with a similar client or a mention of a challenge this decision maker might face. This shows you know their business.*

Seller: I'm calling because I'd like to talk to Jack about some of the challenges your organization is facing related to...

- Or: I was talking to Joe Thompson in your R&D department. He suggested that I speak with Jack.

- Or: I have some ideas I'd like to run by Jack regarding how your company can...

> ***If you don't have all the information like the decision maker's name, elicit the gatekeeper's help. The more you can engage the gatekeeper in the process, the better.***

Getting past the gatekeeper is not always easy and it often takes time and persistence. Duane Cummings, a successful business owner, former world-class professional soccer player and coach and consultant to some of the world's best-known athletes and business owners shares this story about getting past the gatekeeper:

"There was a company that no one in our company was able to get into. They were already working with a competitor and were locked up tight. I didn't care. I had another customer just down the road and every time I visited them, I visited the other company too.

Now this was the typical receptionist behind a glass window, if you don't have an appointment, they can't see you now, she won't give you extension numbers, won't put you through on voice mail, none of that stuff, she was in the true sense of the word the 'gatekeeper.' So the lady's probably in her late 50's, early 60's, sitting in her little window, and the first time I go in there I drop off my card and I joke with her, saying something like, 'Our company has never sold you anything, but I'm a salesman, and I gotta feed my family, and sooner or later I gotta crack a new egg,' or something like that. And she sort of laughs, she's cordial, but it was one of those smiles that said, 'No sale is ever going to happen here.'

It was close to the holidays, and I noticed she had three or four little bitty snowmen on her desk. So a week later, when I stopped by again, I brought her a snowman. I said something like, 'People come in here all the time and they're trying to get to people past you, they're trying to take them to lunch, trying to take them to golf, trying to sell them something. Our company has never sold you anything anyway so I'm just going to stop by because you're a nice person, you smile and you're cordial to me every time I come in. I need more people in my life like that.' So she smiled and took my snowman. Although it was genuine, her smile again said, 'No sale.'

So then I come back around for New Year's and I brought a little celebration packet with a party hat, one of those noisemakers and such, and I said, 'I hope you have a great celebration and I hope next year is a great year for you.' She took the party packet and said, 'You know you don't have to keep coming in here giving me things.' I told her, 'I come a block away from here anyway, you're in my industry, it would be silly of me not to come in here and treat you well. Someday my competitors might win the lottery and retire and you're going to need product, and I'll still be standing here and sooner or later someone will call me."

Duane is obviously in this for the long haul. He understands that patient persistence pays. He continues to stop by, saying hello, occasionally bringing gifts that make the gatekeeper feel appreciated. Now it's Valentine's Day and on this holiday Duane always brings a rose to every receptionist, every gatekeeper in his world. So he once again sees the receptionist behind the window and brings her a rose. Duane says,

"The day after Valentine's Day I get an email from the owner of the company asking me to see him when I stop by next time. It was kind of a short, almost terse email and I thought maybe I was going to get chewed out for getting his receptionist a flower. Of course I'd already checked out the company and the owner online, but there was no LinkedIn profile picture, no articles about him, he seemed kind of a recluse. But I also knew he was loyal to his vendors, and if I ever got in there he would be loyal to me. So I'm escorted into his office and I sit and wait. A couple minutes later the receptionist and the owner walk in together and I thought 'Oh boy, it is about the flower.' And then the owner proceeds to tell me the receptionist, the gatekeeper, is his mother!"

You can probably guess the rest. The owner told Duane,

"I have never had anyone be so nice to my mom and treat her with so much respect, so much dignity, even though they weren't getting anything out of it. You continue to come here even though you didn't think you would sell anything, you didn't look past my mother."

The next year, that company became Duane's number one account.

The Wizard Answered the Phone. Now What?

Occasionally an executive will answer their own phone. When you focus before the call, *practice* and are prepared, you succeed in having an engaging conversation. When you don't FOCUS this could happen:

> *"Taking a look at my top ten list my eyes zeroed in on the number one prospect. I reviewed my perfectly crafted script, took a deep breath and dialed. The phone rang. I stood up – erect, with good posture to ensure the best possible voice quality. It rang again. I smiled to ensure I sounded approachable – personable. It rang again. 'This is Peter,' the voice said in a brisk British accent. I waited for the voice mail to continue, ready to deliver my message at the sound of the beep. There was a pause – a long, silent pause.*
>
> *Suddenly, I realized I was actually speaking to the vice president of sales and marketing. These bigwigs never answer their own phones in the middle of the day. My mind went totally blank. Everything I had planned to say disappeared. Words came pouring out of my mouth. I bumbled. I stumbled. I sounded about as stupid as anyone could possibly sound. Sure enough the VP quickly cut in and put me out of my misery, 'We handle all that internally,' he said. Normally I'd take that comment in stride and neutralize it without missing a beat. Instead all I wanted to do was to get off the phone as soon as humanly possible. 'Thank you for your time,' I said, and quickly hung up the phone."*

This is an actual conversation Jill Konrath, author of *Selling to Big Companies* had.

Even the most seasoned conversationalists have moments when things fall apart. It's after those situations that one must reflect and ask, "How am I going to do better next time?"

Jill goes on to say,

"Connecting with a real decision maker can easily be perceived as a 'do or die' situation. Fortunately, it's not. They forget about you even before they've hung up. You can try again in another month."

When you reach the decision maker: Don't say, *"I'll only take up two minutes of your time."*

"First off, nothing takes two minutes. Second, you're worth more than two minutes," as communication coach, Bill McGowan points out in his book, *Pitch Perfect: How to Say It Right the First Time, Every Time.*

Here's a terrific opening line Bill recommends when you're speaking directly to the decision maker:

"Hi, John, it's (your name) and I know we're both juggling crazy schedules, so I'll get right to the point."

This allows you to acknowledge that the executive is busy while recognizing that you are too.

Remember our tips from the gatekeeper section? First FOCUS and be prepared for the conversation by using one of these topic openers:

- *Referral you received from someone in the company or outside*

- *Your expertise and how you worked with the competition*

- *Article or something of interest that you uncovered that could apply to their company*

Here's an example of how a friendly referral turned into a fabulous way to get a CEO conversation started:

> *"While in California I played a round of golf with a ladies group. When asked about my business I said I owned a market research company and a woman quickly commented, 'Very interesting. My son is the CEO of a large NY ad agency.' I asked for and she happily gave me his contact information. When I reached him I opened our conversation with the fun time I had playing golf with his mom."*
> *~ Debbie Silverman*

Granted, the CEO's mom being the referral source provided an advantage. The lesson is the same, and that's to look for areas of interest to that high level person. For example, a client recently researched a CEO of a bank he wanted to get into. Tom found out the CEO and he shared the same alma mater at around the same time and wrote that in his email subject. The CEO called *HIM*.

> **In the absence of a referral or introduction, look for common ground.**

Just like in the Wizard of Oz, when Dorothy and her friends had the information they needed, speaking with the Wizard resulted in them all getting what they wanted.

Get Out of the Cold

Cold calling is in the past. Yes. It's a dinosaur. Just the sound of the words "Cold Call" sends shivers down our spines. In today's world we have gold at our fingertips in that there's an abundance of information available about almost anyone. LinkedIn, Facebook, Google, Pinterest, et al, allow us to learn about people before we even meet them. And after we meet them, it gives us a way to stay in touch.

> **Whether you're contacting someone for the first time, following up with someone you met yesterday or six months ago, use technology to turn that cold lead into a warm one.**

Nancy Matthews, author, speaker, business strategist and Founder of Women's Prosperity Network shares these easy strategies for warming up cold contacts:

1. What do you know about the person or group you are about to call?

Even if you've never met, the Internet is the perfect resource tool to learn about your prospect. Start by Googling them, and then head to social media for more info. *(I just love how Google is now a verb!)*

2. Look for clues to build rapport and find their 'hot buttons.'

Anyone in sales knows that building rapport is the first step in the sales process. What do you have in common with them to start a warm conversation based on commonalities rather than a cold call out of the blue? The receptionist who answers the phone is more likely to put you through to the head honcho and decision maker if you can quickly get to the bottom line of what's in it for them. You've got to know what it is they want (by doing some research first) to be able to concisely convey that message.

3. **Engage in *their* sales process**.

    Sign up for their newsletter or free course. Today most businesses offer some entry level way of getting to know more about them directly on their website. When you engage in their process you receive two great benefits: first, you let them know you're interested in them; and second, you become familiar with their culture and way of doing business. Both of these benefits allow you to make a warm call instead of a cold call.

We understand that some of you may be reading this and are thinking, *"I don't have time to do all that up front work. I just need to bang through as many cold calls as possible. I know the statistics …1 in 100…"*

For those of you that like making 100 cold calls to find the needle in the haystack, go right ahead. But for those of you who **prefer quality over quantity**, we invite you to take a few extra minutes on the front end to reap huge rewards on the back end. Create your own statistic. Use information marketing to your advantage and turn cold calls into warm connections that lead to fast results and increased revenue!

> **Think of sales as artistry – you are creating a work of art in building relationships with your prospects and clients.**

The Fortune is in the Follow Up

Once you've made the connection, whether through a cold call or an introduction, understand that you are just getting started. It is unusual for someone to buy the first time they meet you and there are many reasons why most people need further prodding: lack of time, too many other things on their mind, cost concerns, cash-flow issues, not sure of the value yet, and even simple inertia. This is reality – which is why follow up is crucial to sales success.

What is amazing is how many times someone shows interest in something and they don't buy at that moment for one reason or another and then they never hear from the sales person again. How crazy is that?! I tell you I like your product and then you disappear?!

People and companies who do not follow up are leaving money on the table. Bottom line, success takes persistence. Research shows that 48% of people NEVER follow up. Moreover, most people stop after getting just ONE "No." Consider these statistics:

- 25% of sales people make a second contact and stop

- 12% of sales people make only 3 contacts and stop

- **Only 10% of sales people make more than 3 contacts**

We get it. It's not fun to hear "No." The key is to be clear on whether you're hearing "No, not now," or "No, not ever." Most people make the assumption that "No" means "Never" and that just isn't true. Studies show:

2% of sales are made on the 1st contact

3% are made on the 2nd contact

5% are made on the 3rd contact

10% are made on the 4th contact

80% are made on the 5th to the 12th contact

This tells us that the sale goes to the few who follow up; the few who are patient and pleasantly persistent. So how do you follow up?

Here are a variety of ways to keep you in front of your prospects:

- Send a "Nice to Meet You" note. Email is OK, hand-written and sent in snail mail is even better.

- Regularly interact with them on Social Media.

- Invite them to lunch, coffee, dinner, networking, a workshop, an event.

- Pay attention to their likes and dislikes. Keep an eye out for quotes, articles, information on areas that interest them and share.

- Call just to connect and say hello.

- Share information about their industry and/or a particular business challenge they're facing.

- Ask their opinion on something you're working on.

Ultimately, the goal is to get an appointment to uncover their needs, make a proposal, create a relationship and do business. That can happen the first time you talk or the tenth time. In your conversations, ask questions to find out their challenges and their needs and ask for an opportunity to solve them.

Now that you've made an appointment to solve their challenge, your follow up is to ensure that you actually meet. Studies show that on average 30% of the time, sales presentation appointments are postponed or cancelled.

Here are 6 tactics to ensure success:

1. Be Specific & Get Commitment for the Follow-Up

The single biggest oversight sales people make is not establishing a specific day and time for the follow up call. Vague commitments such as *"Call me next week,"* or *"I'll send you a proposal and follow up in a few days,"* results in missed calls, voice mails and a longer sales cycle. Instead say,

> *"I'm happy to put together a proposal and email it to you by Wednesday. I recommend we get together on the phone Tuesday the 16th or Wednesday the 17th to review it in detail and determine any next steps. Which day works best for you, Tuesday or Wednesday?"*

> *Always offer choices, it gives the prospect the feeling of control, e.g., "Which works for you, Monday or Thursday?"*

2. Email a Reminder the Day Before the Meeting

The day before your meeting, send an email reminding them of the appointment. Your subject line should be: "Confirming our Appointment Tomorrow." The subject line reminds them of the appointment and is vague enough that the person will probably open it to make sure the time is right and the appointment is still on.

> *Keep your subject line vague enough to ensure they open your email.*

In your email, let them know what to expect in the meeting:

> *"Susan, the call should take only about 10 minutes. We'll review the proposal to reduce your costs and increase your customer satisfaction. I'll answer any questions and we'll determine next steps, if any."*

These words echo what was said when the appointment was originally set. Notice the phrase, "...determine next steps, if any," which helps reduce some of the pressure or concern a first time buyer may have. Often people skip the appointment because they are concerned about making a commitment to buy. It's natural and OK. If you are informal and easygoing they are more likely to actually show up for the appointment.

> *Do your homework. Look for articles online and offline relative to your market, to business in general, and for personal areas of interest. Keep a file of these articles -- they can be used over and over again.*

3. Add Value

People successful at relationship building know to be aware of their prospect's interests and be on the lookout for articles, stories and information of interest to them. When you do, you can attach something else with the appointment reminder. That something else may be the thing that makes them open your email.

Add "and an article on (area of interest) for you" to your subject line and at the end of your e-mail add a P.S. that says, *"Susan, I ran across this fascinating article about (area of interest) and I know you'll find some great ideas in it."*

It can be about any area of interest you uncovered in your previous contact(s), personal or business. This creates value even if they don't read it. Why? Because you went over and above, you did that little extra that make people EXTRA-ordinary. It helps you be remembered and gives the prospect another good reason to do business with you.

4. Call On Time

Start off on the right foot. Show that you have integrity and that you do what you say you'll do. Call on time. Always be early, or exactly on time for an appointment, especially this all-important one. Do not be late, not even by a minute.

When you show respect by being on time, it speaks volumes about you, your company and your products and services.

5. Make a Strong Opening Statement that Gets to the Benefits

Don't make a generic, boring, vanilla opening statement such as:

- "I'm calling to follow up on the proposal I sent."

- "I'm calling to see if you had any questions."

- "I want to make sure you got my e-mail."

- "I'm calling to see if you made a decision."

It's not that these statements aren't good; it's just that they're so common. They don't position you or differentiate you. Be unique, be powerful in your introduction and your presentation will follow.

Open Your Conversation Powerfully

Remind them why you're calling; repeat the challenge points so the issues are once again in front of them.

Pat: *"Nancy, this is Pat Jones from ABC Merchant Services. When we talked last week you told me you had two immediate concerns: 1) you're concerned that your merchant services costs are too high, and 2) you're dissatisfied with the customer service in resolving problems because it ultimately causes irritation to your customers. You said you are worried about losing business over it."*

Pat reminds Nancy why she agreed to hearing this proposal in the first place. Why is this necessary? Because Pat knows that people are busy, that they forget, or that the urgency from last week may be diminished this week. So she reminds Nancy that she's got a problem she wants to solve and what those problems are.

Remind your prospect of the irritation they're experiencing and then give them a roadmap of the call, tell them what they can expect.

> Pat: *"I'd like to recommend 2 things. First let's review your costs and compare them to the pricing we are offering and second, let's take a look at the customer service options that will keep you happy and your customers coming back. Then we'll determine next steps, if any. Does that work for you?"*

People like a clear, concise understanding of what's happening next. They want to work with people who are organized and who value their time by moving the conversation forward. It gives them confidence in you, your company and your ability to meet their needs.

6. Be Persistent, Patiently Polite and Professional

When you follow these steps, most of the time your prospect will show up for the appointment and you'll have the opportunity to make a sale. Approximately 30% of the time, they won't show up. If the person isn't there, leave a message so they know you called on time. Say something like:

> Pat: *"Hi Nancy, it's Pat from ABC Merchant Services calling for our 9:00 appointment. It looks like you're tied*

up for a few minutes. I'll call back at 9:15 if I haven't heard from you. My number is _____. Looking forward to talking."

Call back in exactly 15 minutes and If they're still not available leave a message. With a smile say:

> *"Hi Nancy, it's Pat from ABC Merchant Services following up on our 9:00 appointment. Looks like you're still tied up.*
> *Please give me a call when you're free. My number is_____. I'll try you again this afternoon."*

This keeps you professional and persistent without being a pest. Give the person a chance to call you back.

> **A half day is time enough to wait for a call back and it makes you seem committed and organized.**

If you still don't reach them, leave another message:

Pat: *"Hi Nancy it's Pat from ABC Merchant Services. I called a couple of times today and we haven't been able to connect. When we spoke last week you said you are concerned that your merchant services costs are too high and that the poor customer service is causing you to lose business. I know that you want to stop paying too much and have a better solution. I have a few new ideas that may work for you. So my number is _____. I look forward to connecting with you."*

Notice how she reminded Nancy about the reason she wants to talk to Pat, about the challenge she still has and invited her to consider that Pat has something different to offer. She did it without embarrassing her or making her feel guilty for missing the appointment. In essence, Pat wants Nancy to think, *"Hmm... I wonder what she has in mind. Guess I'll call and find out because I really need a solution."*

What if she still doesn't return the call?

> *Continue following up. Be persistent and spread your calls far enough apart so that the person doesn't feel stalked. Make 4 or 5 more follow up calls and space them 3 days apart the first time, 5 the next, 7 after that and so on. If there's no response by then, pat yourself on the back for being consistent and persistent and make a follow up call again in 30 days.*

Until you reach them and are told, "NO, I'm not interested and I never will be," keep going and going and going, spacing your follow up calls 30, 60, 90 days apart. Continue relationship building with the follow up tips provided at the beginning of this section.

Stay patient, pleasant, professional and persistent.
Learn more about maximizing your relationship with your client or customer and how to delight them by accelerating your understanding of their needs:

Go to http://Consumer-Perspective.com
and download your free e-book
"7 Secrets to Catapulting Your Business."

Don't Close that Sale Worksheet

Remember, the goal of the conversation is to open or create a relationship. As you plan for the sale, **FOCUS:**

F: FINISH FIRST: What is the outcome you want to achieve?

_____

_____

_____

O: OBSERVE: You can observe something about the person you're about to speak with by doing some detective work online. Check out the person or company on Google, LinkedIn, Facebook and other Social Media and resources.

Write at least three facts about the person with whom you are creating a relationship:

1._____

2._____

3._____

Write at least three facts about the person's company. Look at their mission statement on their website to find their higher values:

1._____

2._____

3._____

C: CLARIFY: Prepare possible questions before you have your conversation.

Write at least three questions to learn more about their challenge points. Use these challenge points when you schedule conversations or meetings:

1._____

_____

2._____

_____

3._____

_____

U: USE THE INFORMATION you learned and practice in the mirror speaking to gatekeepers. Practice that conversation as though you're speaking with the decision maker.

S: STAY IN THE MOMENT: Practice staying in the moment before you get to the conversation. Practice using the technique we mentioned earlier: Think of a person, place or thing. Really focus on that particular thought. Now let your mind wander to another person, place or thing. When you feel your mind shifting to another thought, say to yourself, 'stay in the moment' and take your mind back to the original thought.

Download a copy of this worksheet at:
http://ItsJustaConversationBook.com/downloads

Negotiation 101

"I'm going to make him an offer he can't refuse."
~Vito Corleone, The Godfather

In This Chapter:
- Setting the Bargaining Table
- Table Manners
- Play the Game
- Win-Win Negotiating

Setting the Bargaining Table

If you're in business, you're a negotiator. Business doesn't happen unless two or more people enter into a transaction. Negotiation skills are essential to business success. It's especially important to master this skill. In her *Seattle Business Magazine* article, *Table Manners* author and CEO advisor, Karen Hough reports, *"on average, women leave more* than *$500K on the table during the course of their careers."* If women are known to be bargain hunters and bill payers, why is this happening? ***"It's happening because women fail to negotiate,"*** says Karen. Before they get to the bargaining table, good negotiators **FOCUS**:

F: FINISH FIRST: Consider what you want the outcome to be, begin with the end in mind. *Know your* **alternatives**. According to Roger Fisher and William Ury, authors of the bestseller *Getting to Yes*, *"The optimal way to evaluate any proposed deal is to weigh it against your best option in the absence of a deal – what's often called the 'best alternative to a negotiated agreement.'"*

> *The value or cost of this alternative helps determine your reservation price, the most you would pay, or the least you would take, to make a deal.*

F also stands for **FACTS**. Use facts not feelings.

"The most difficult thing in any negotiation, almost, is making sure that you strip it of the emotion and deal with the facts." ~ Former Senator Howard Baker

> *Keep negotiations factual. No language such as "I believe" or "I think." Stick with FACTS.*

O: OBSERVE: Pay attention and listen.

Know your counterpart. A deep understanding of your counterpart's interests and motives helps you evaluate their strengths and weaknesses and gives you a sense of the bargaining zone, which lies between your reservation price and theirs.

Research your counterpart and imagine yourself in their shoes. *"The better able you are to get inside the head of your opponent, the better your negotiated outcomes are likely to be,"* says Adam D. Galinsky, Professor at Northwestern University's Kellogg School of Management.

"A negotiator should observe everything. You must be part Sherlock Holmes and part Sigmund Freud," said Victor Kiam, *(U.S. businessman who became famous for his advert saying "I liked the shaver so much, I bought the company" – Remington razors).*

C: CLARIFY what's needed before you get to the bargaining table. Know the standards and accepted norms, spoken or not. Find out as much as you can about everything. It's like checking the *Kelly Blue Book* for used car prices. You may even have an advantage because you have better information. And, be sure to clarify by asking questions.

Women may have an advantage when it comes to questions. Their ability to engage people in conversation and their curiosity about what others need often leads to better negotiations.

C also stands for Calm. Remain **CALM** throughout the negotiation.

U: UNIQUE: Be yourself. And, match and mirror (as best you can) to create rapport.

S: STAY IN THE MOMENT: By staying in the moment you can control the pace of the negotiation.

> *Stay calm, patient and collected.*

You can negotiate for what you want by simply outlasting someone else. If you have patience, use it. If you lack patience, gain it. What often happens in negotiations is that people get tired and accept a position they wouldn't ordinarily accept because they're tired of negotiating. When you can outlast someone by staying at the table longer, chances are you'll get more of what you want.

Again, women may have an advantage here. They generally tend to be more patient than men. This personality trait, when used properly, can mean the difference between walking away from the negotiating table happy or not. Develop patience!

S also stands for *Silence.* Silence is an effective negotiating tactic. When the other party makes a proposal or offer, don't reply immediately. Instead use your body language, facial expression and/or the sound of silence to indicate you're not satisfied. This will make the other person feel uncomfortable and insecure and often make them come up with a better offer to fill the silence.

> *Ditch the 4-Second Rule. In negotiations, the longer the silence, the better. Here, we recommend the 10-Second Rule.*

Table Manners

Face-to-Face or Remote?

You may have heard that it's always best to negotiate face-to-face. After all, the key dimensions of communication are available in person: body language, facial expressions, tonality and your words.

And while this is true, there are good points to make for both face-to-face and remote negotiations.

Face-to Face

- Face-to-face meetings are important when the parties don't know each other and need to establish rapport.

- Face-to-face negotiations tend to be more civilized, with more concessions made and a higher likelihood of reaching a successful agreement.

- *"Face-to-face negotiations favor the powerful,"* according to Michael Taylor of Imperial College London. CEO's and other high level people know and embrace the art of negotiation. After all, they probably wouldn't be where they are today if it weren't for their superior negotiation skills.

Your Place or Mine?

Most people presume there is a home-court advantage in negotiation, and there is some evidence to back that up. Still, there are often good reasons to take the talks to your counterpart's table. Michael Rainey, a dispute resolution practitioner who teaches at Pepperdine University offers the following:

"Playing an away game – Negotiating on your opponent's turf signals respect and accommodation tempered with confidence. It gives you an opportunity to gather intelligence about your counterpart and the culture in which he or she operates. Finally, it makes it harder for the other side to claim, 'the file's at the office.' Home-field advantage – If your office walls reflect power or influence that you want to impress upon your counterpart, conducting the negotiations within them will send that message. And, your opponent will have the same advantage you would have at his or her site."

Seating Arrangements

Behaviorists say that negotiating across a table can produce a defensive, competitive or even combative atmosphere.

> **Working at the corner of the table, or with your counterpart at your side, creates a collaborative environment.**

Remote

Remote negotiations include video conferencing, telephone, email or letter, and negotiation by proxy (or mediator).

If a real time, in-person, face-to-face meeting is not possible, the next best scenario may be **video conferencing**.

With video conferencing, negotiators finally have an advantage, giving them access to the non-verbal communication necessary for reading the prospect and meeting potential customers, partners and competitors in their comfort zone, online.

Look for a video conferencing service that's easy to use for you and the other parties.

> *Successful negotiators know how to close the deal and leave the prospect feeling the emotions of the moment; people buy from emotion and back it up with logic.*

Even in a remote situation, you can influence them to sign the deal right in the meeting. You can have them download the agreement right in the room, print and sign it and then upload it right back into your video meeting room.

Telephone

If you're unable to meet in person and video conferencing is not an option, then the telephone can work. It works even better if you already have a good relationship and there has already been face-to-face contact.

Since body language and eye contact are not part of the equation in a telephone negotiation, pay special attention to the voice tone and outside sounds (on your end and theirs).

> *Follow your instincts and be prepared to walk away when the negotiation isn't going the way you planned or when you have an uncomfortable feeling about it.*

Here's an example of a phone conversation that didn't go as planned:

"As president of a local chapter of a large women's golf organization I did what I could to negotiate the best prices at local golf courses. There was a gentleman that sold discounted cards that covered 10-15 golf courses – and he was the only game in town – at that time. The card was priced at $285 per person. When I called him, I introduced myself and told him about our chapter and that we have over 150 members. I asked him if he would work with us on the price and that we would guarantee that we would purchase a certain amount of cards. He said, 'We don't work with anyone on the price. The price is what it is – take it or leave it.' **I left it!** *The moral of the story is just because someone appears to have the upper hand in a negotiation it doesn't mean you have to take the offer. Be prepared to walk away!"*

While I walked away from that negotiation, I used what I'd experienced, learned and took it to the next conversation. Here's how that went:

"I was speaking with a tournament director of a local golf course who wanted our business and has a lot of very important contacts and relationships. He asked me, 'What can we do to get your business?' I told him about my conversation and experience with the discount golf card company owner and said that I will never buy a discount card from him. I asked the tournament director if there was anything he could do and he said he would look into it. What came out of this negotiation conversation was amazing! The tournament director and the owner of the golf course created a fabulous offer. They offered to purchase the discount cards and provide each of our

members with a **free** card (savings of $285 per person) if we agreed to play the course a certain number of times during the year. This 'deal' was so well received that we were able to grow our chapter by 34%. It truly was a win-win situation for my members and the golf course."

The key point is that the golf tournament director and owner listened to their prospect. They took that information and successfully negotiated for the business.

Email or Letter

Negotiation by email, text or letter further separates the parties such that they do not have to speak to one another.

This method is not recommended unless it is the only way to finalize the deal. Because there's a delay, there's time for careful consideration, research and consultation with others. However, it also stretches out the conversation over a longer time. Another negative to this approach is that the written word may be misconstrued and negotiations could fall apart.

Negotiation by Proxy

A proxy is an intermediary, a person who takes your demands and offers and communicates them to the other person. The proxy may be a mutual acquaintance, a lawyer, a mediator or some other person. This may be necessary if the parties are already in conflict or where trust is low.

In negotiation by proxy, the parties may never meet or even know who they are. This can lead to stereotyping, objectification and other caricaturing of each other, which can lead to further problems.

Where negotiation by proxy can work well is when the proxy, who must be trusted by both parties, acts as a trust substitute and facilitates an equitable agreement.

Play the Game

First impressions make a difference. Getting off to a good start in business negotiations will likely influence the final agreement. When you focus and are prepared you'll succeed at the negotiation game.

In his article in "International Trade Forum Magazine," *Business Negotiations: Making the First Offer*, Claude Cellich, VP of International University in Geneva says, *"A successful negotiation starts with asking these three questions before making an opening offer*:

1. Who should make the first offer? Should it be high or low?

2. What should you do if your opening offer is not accepted?

3. What should you do if your opening offer is rejected?"

Claude goes on to say, *"Some negotiators recommend letting the other side open the discussions while others suggest that making the first offer gives you a tactical advantage."*

The following guidelines from *Business Negotiations: Making the First Offer*,[3] say that for the best negotiations, the opening offer should:

---

[3] *Parts excerpted from Business Negotiations: Making the First Offer, by Claude Cellich, VP of the International University in Geneva, International Trade Forum Magazine*

- Stress mutual benefits

- Be clear and positive

- Imply flexibility

- Create interest

- Demonstrate confidence

- Promote goodwill

1. Should I make the first offer?

Yes, if you wish to take the initiative and set the tone of the discussions. By making the first move you establish a reference or anchor point.

Your anchor point will probably influence the other side's responses. The other party now knows your position, and will either accept it, reject it or request a counter-offer.

At this point, don't make unnecessary concessions; seek clarifications instead. This approach implies that your initial offer is based on recent market information, is credible and presented with conviction.

No, do not make the first offer if you are not familiar with the market in which you want to do business. Making an offer without adequate information or a clear understanding of what the other side wants places you in a risky position.

For example, having your first offer accepted could mean that you have underestimated the market. One way around this is to ask what budget is available for the project before you offer.

Another reason for not making the first offer, even if you have the market information, is to test the seriousness of the other side, particularly if it is a new business deal.

"I recently negotiated a lump sum payment on a debt owed to me that I'd been chasing for almost 6 months. The likelihood of court was looming large. I didn't want to spend the time, energy or money to litigate so I was willing to accept 50%. I invited them to make the first offer to see how serious they were. They came in at 65% making for an easy win-win negotiation."
  ~ Trish Carr

2. Should I open high?

Yes. Make an aggressive first offer if you can justify the level of your offer.

> *Think big and don't be afraid to ask largely. We're going to repeat this one –*
> *THINK BIG AND DON'T BE AFRAID TO ASK LARGELY.*

When you ask largely, good things happen. Remember Debbie Silverman asking the 7-figure business coach for four leads?

"At Women's Prosperity Network's Un-Conference, we were invited to ask a panel of experts a question — I asked a renowned 7-figure business coach for four of his best leads. He said 'Four is too many.' I went on to build rapport with him and then he asked, 'Would one lead do?'

If I only asked for one in the beginning, he may have said 'no' and I would have walked away with none."

Starting high is common in markets where business executives rate their superior negotiating skills by how many concessions they get. By starting high it gives you a place to go. When presenting an offer be careful that it may be considered so high by the other side that it results in a deadlock.

Remember, when you start with a high offer be prepared to justify it.

2a. Should I open low?

Yes, in special situations. Skilled negotiators may make a low initial offer, near the bottom line – not so much to get the business, but to be invited to the negotiations.

When they hope to enter into new markets or to get a foot in the door with a new customer, business executives often open with a proposal that is close to, or below their bottom line. In such cases, it is vital to explain that the offer is valid for a limited time only.

> *"I've seen low offers a lot in the advertising world when an agency wants to be part of a new business pitch."*
> *~Debbie Silverman*

> **When facing strong competition, your offer should be more or less in line with theirs.**

3. What should I do if my first offer is not accepted?

React positively. Like in the sales conversation, a "No" should be regarded as the beginning of the negotiations, not a time to make concessions or take a defensive attitude.

Experienced negotiators expect questions. They turn objections into opportunities, without getting into concessions.

> ***Consider each objection as an ideal way to start an information exchange through questioning.***

Claude offers the following for handling common comments to first offers:

They say:
"Your offer is too expensive."

You say:
"What do you consider acceptable and on what basis?"
Ask yourself: "If I'm too expensive, why is the other side negotiating with me?"

They say:
"We don't have that kind of budget."

Find out how large the budget is and for what time frame. Explore whether your offer can fit within the overall budget by checking whether the other side can combine several budget lines. Propose deferred payment schedules to show you want to work with them. You can also split the order into smaller units to meet current budget limitations.

They say:
"That's not what we are looking for."

You say:
"What specifically are you looking for?"

Find out which aspects of your offer they like best. Keep asking questions until you have a clear understanding of the other side's real needs then change your offer in light of the new information received.

They say:
"Your offer is not competitive."

You say:
"Please help me understand, why isn't my offer competitive?

Find out if your competitors' offers are comparable to yours. Look for less strong qualities in the other offers and emphasize your strengths. Reformulate your offer by not making direct comparisons with competition. Focus on the unique features and benefits of your products or services.

> ***Know how high or low you are willing to go and if it's not attained, be prepared to WALK AWAY!***

Win-Win Negotiating

"In an ideal world, a win-win agreement is the only kind of deal that would ever close. Even in today's world, the vast majority of negotiations end in win-win situations."
~Michael C. Donaldson, Negotiating for Dummies

When you've reached the end of a negotiation and no one has walked away, the best outcome for both parties is a "win-

win" situation where both parties leave happy. And while that's the best outcome, **it is not your responsibility to make sure the other party's goals are met.** This is especially important for women to remember because in general women are concerned more about the other person's welfare. (Yes, we recognize it's a generality and that men experience this too.)

> *FOCUS on your goal and*
> *the outcome you want to achieve.*

In *Negotiating for Dummies*, Michael Donaldson goes on to suggest that if, before closing, you can answer "Yes" to the following questions, most likely you've made a win-win deal:

- Does the agreement further your personal long-range goals?

- Does the outcome of the negotiation fit into your vision statement?

- Does the agreement fall comfortably within the goals and limits that you set for this particular negotiation?

- Can you perform your side of the agreement to the fullest?

- Do you intend to meet your commitment?

- Based on all the information, can the other side perform the agreement to your expectations?

- Based on what you know, does the other side intend to carry out the terms of the agreement?

Here is an excellent example of a successful negotiation:

Lessons from "The Godfather"

If you recall the iconic movie, *The Godfather*, there was a short scene where the protagonist, Michael Corleone, was negotiating with Las Vegas casino owner, Mo Green, to buy into the business. Michael's father was nearly killed and their family was under attack in New York, so they needed to move their headquarters. Michael's older brother, Fredo, lived in Vegas and worked for Mo Green. During the negotiation, there was an obvious emotional contrast between Michael and Mo. Throughout the discussion as Mo got all in a lather, Michael remained completely *calm.*

Research shows that emotionally neutral decision makers make better decisions. Hsee & Rottenstreich's 2004 study in *The Journal of Experimental Psychology,* found that emotional thinking impairs discrimination. Druckman and Olekalns 2008 similar study also claims that negative emotions have an adverse effect when negotiating.

> *The more emotional you are in a situation, the less likely you are to maximize outcomes in decision making.*

The second negotiation technique Michael Corleone used was to keep *silent.* Mo argued aggressively while Michael stayed silent and spoke only a few words. Michael's silence put Mo under pressure and made him rush the process. Michael waited patiently until Mo showed his hand about a deal with a rival family. Michael then dropped the clincher, "Is that why you slapped my brother around in public?" Michael waited for the right moment to say he knew his brother was mistreated. (It's not a good idea to beat up the Godfather's son!) And he used that key information as leverage to get what he wanted.

In a negotiation, just because you have all the information, doesn't mean you lay it all on the table at once. Pick your spots; use the information at the right time.

Michael Corleone did his homework before the negotiation. He knew everything about the operation down to the working relationship between Mo and his brother. He knew exactly what buttons to push to take it over.

> *The more information you have, the better deal you can make.*

Negotiation 101 Worksheet

When done properly, both parties walk away from the negotiating table winners. As you plan for the negotiation remember to ~~FOCUS.~~

F: FINISH FIRST: What is the perfect outcome you want to achieve? (If you are in a position to ask largely, do so!)

_____

_____

_____

_____

O: OBSERVE: You can observe something about the person you are negotiating with by doing some detective work online. Check out the person or company on Google, LinkedIn and/or Facebook.

Write at least three facts about the person or company that you can use to your advantage during the negotiation:

1._____

2._____

3._____

Identify two or more competitors and do your research to learn what they are proposing:

Competitor #1_____

Competitor #2_____

C: CLARIFY: Prepare three possible questions before you start your negotiation. Be prepared to handle a negative response to price or whatever you are negotiating about:

1._____
2._____
3._____

U: USE THE INFORMATION you learned and practice in the mirror or with an associate. Practice patience and the 10-Second Rule of Silence.

S: STAY IN THE MOMENT: You can practice staying in the moment before you get to the negotiation. When practicing with an associate, see how much you are actually listening and how much you are thinking ahead. If your mind starts to think ahead, bring yourself back by saying, "Stay in the Moment."

Download a copy of this worksheet at:
http://ItsJustaConversationBook.com/downloads

Chapter Five

Employees and Bosses and Salaries, Oh My

*"There's no way I can justify my salary level, but I'm
learning to live with it."*
~ Drew Carey

In This Chapter:
- Big Job Interview?
- Let's Talk Money
- Get Engaged
- You're Fired!

*"To increase your chances of getting your
resume to the top of the pile and be invited in
for the interview, cut and paste key phrases
from the position description, add it to the
bottom of your resume in a tiny size font
using white font so it appears as hidden."*

"...this may trip up an ATS system (Applicant Tracking System) which picks up key words in your resume that fit the job description," says Carrie Florea, Ph.D, Talent Acquisition and Behavior Specialist.

Big Job Interview?

Few people actually like interviewing for a new job. For some, the anxiousness they feel is right up there with selling and negotiating. And that's no surprise because it's actually the same thing. After all, you are selling yourself and you have to negotiate your salary and benefits along the way.

Remember that a job interview is simply a conversation and remember to **FOCUS**:

F: FINISH FIRST: Think in reverse and consider how you want the interview to go.

O: OBSERVE AND LISTEN: Know your interviewer. Get in touch with your friend Google and check out the company and the person with whom you'll be interviewing. Remember to observe their office when you're there so you can better understand their passions, hobbies and interests and build rapport with them.

> *Listen to the interviewer. The more the interviewer talks the more you learn about the company and how you can make a difference.*

C: CLARIFY the job and your position by asking questions. According to managers and directors of various companies, when prospects ask the interviewer questions it shows that they're truly interested in the job, the company and how they can make a difference. Some questions to consider:

- What is an example of a client challenge you have recently faced?

- Where do you see the company going in the next five years?

- What is the question you really want to ask me but haven't?

- What impact would I have on the team when I'm hired?

- What would make someone really successful in this role?

When you ask some or all of these questions, be prepared for silence on the other end, you may surprise the interviewer with your level of interest.

C also stands for **CALM**. Remain CALM throughout the interview. To feel calm and look relaxed, remember to breathe and use:

> *The 4 by 4 Technique:*
> *Inhale for 4 seconds through your nose; hold for 4 seconds; exhale for 4 seconds through your mouth and hold that for 4 seconds. Repeat two or three times until you feel calm.*

"When I interview prospective candidates, I always look for their ability to think on their feet. The last thing I need in my organization is someone who can't think and move quickly."
   ~Trish Carr

> **Don't memorize answers to possible questions – practice your responses to get comfortable with them and make sure you sound authentic.**

> **Turn off your negative self-talk and create a new, positive message instead.**

When you have a negative conversation with *yourself* and you catch yourself thinking things like, "I'm not sure I can do this," or "I may not be qualified," STOP and take a deep breath. In *Crazy Good Interviewing*, John Molidor and Barbara Parus suggest that you *"Change your negative self-talk to 'I am here to share to the best of my ability and that is all I can really do."*

> **Prepare ahead of time.**

"For most of my career, every time I went on a job interview, I got the job. If I wanted it, I did my homework and found out everything I could about it. I also made sure that for every quality they were looking for, that I had two

or three examples of how I demonstrated that quality. It's not about listing qualifications, it's about showing how you demonstrate them that counts."
    ~Trish Carr

competing. Rather, turn that energy around and be **creative** in your approach. You will immediately feel more expansive, less constricted. You'll breathe easier and think more clearly. Relax, breathe.

> *Be creative rather than competitive in any business conversation and you'll reap the benefits of this positive energy.*

U: BE UNIQUE and be yourself. And, match and mirror the best you can to build rapport.

Dress appropriately for the position for which you're interviewing. Remember, your clothes are an indication as to whether you're in their 'club' or not.

> *Dress to join their club and accessorize to show your unique personality.*

In *Winning Body Language,* Mark Bowden says,
    "Always follow that person, whether the person is the hiring manager or an assistant, to show you understand protocol. Try to 'mirror' that person's tempo and demeanor — it shows you can easily fit into the environment."

It's Just a Conversation

When interviewing, according to HSM Career Center, one should match the following:

- Voice tone (how you sound), speed and volume

- Breathing rates

- Speech patterns – pick up the key words or phrases your interviewer uses and build these subtly into your conversation. Notice how the interviewer handles information. Do they like detail, or talk about the bigger picture? Feedback information in a similar way

- Rhythm of body movement and energy levels

- Body postures and gestures (don't use this one too often as it can be obvious and may be perceived as mimicking)

> *Matching and mirroring starts on the walk to the interview.*

S: STAY IN THE MOMENT during the interview. Don't let your mind take over so you miss what's being said. By staying in the moment you demonstrate that you are a good listener.

Let's Talk Money

For some people, talking about money and compensation is on par with going to the dentist. Why is it not easy for some and a piece of cake for others?

Let's start with the interviewing process. When you are interviewing for a job, chances are you know the salary range before you go on the interview, right? So, how do you handle the tricky conversation about money?

Salary and Compensation at an Interview

As with any job interview or negotiation, listen and know when to speak and remember to **FOCUS:**

F: FINISH FIRST: Have a salary figure in mind before you get to the interview. Your talent has value. Find out what the salary range is for the job you want. Decide the figure you'd love to get and the figure you would not be interested in taking so that your parameters are clear.

> *Talk to people in your field to get an idea of salary levels. Check out online resources like Salary.com and remember that online sources are not necessarily as accurate as talking to someone with firsthand knowledge.*

O: OBSERVE: Observe what the interviewer shares about the job, the company and anything that gives you more information to support you in getting the job.

> *Let the interviewer bring up salary and compensation.*

C: COUNTER-OFFER: When you do your homework and know what the market is paying, you're in a good position to counter-offer.

> *Know that employers anticipate a counter-offer and most leave room for negotiation in their first offer.*

U: USE GOOD JUDGEMENT and facts when negotiating. Leave the emotion at home.

S: STAY IN THE MOMENT: Remember to listen to the interviewer and not the voice in your head.

When Negotiating Compensation:

- The first offer may not be the best offer. When you accept the first offer you may be leaving money on the table.

- Be prepared. Know how much you want and what the industry standard is for the position.

- Negotiate beyond the base pay. Remember there are other elements to your total salary package, like benefits, understanding performance expectations and minimum severance.

- It's business. Detach your emotions from the conversation.

To strengthen your position at an interview: *Focus on what you can offer the employer. Take a buyer's approach – you can take it or leave it. Have other job options available.*

Asking for a Raise

Asking for a raise can feel as uncomfortable as talking about salary in a job interview.

What's interesting is that some supervisors and managers are just as reluctant to have this conversation as you are.

With the increase in legal issues facing companies regarding fair compensation, managers and supervisors must carefully consider what they say when having any salary conversation.

The best salary conversation is the one where the employee and the manager both end the conversation smiling. This is true for any negotiation. We're always better off with a win-win situation!

The strategies to successfully negotiate a raise in your existing job are the same as the strategies you use when interviewing for the job (as outlined above). Above all, remember to **FOCUS:**

F: FINISH FIRST: Think ahead – have the amount you want in mind. Focus on the outcome you want.

> *I was being evaluated at work for a promotion and VP title. Before I met with my boss I visualized my promotion and what I would be doing in that position. When I met with my boss I spoke confidently and shared ideas on how my promotion would benefit the company – I got the promotion and a raise!*
> *~Debbie Silverman*

O: OBSERVE: Do your research and come to the conversation with specific facts on what you've accomplished and how you have moved the company forward.

C: CLARIFY: Ask clarifying questions to ensure understanding.

U: USE YOUR EXPERIENCE and examples of success to make your points.

S: STAY IN THE MOMENT: Remember to stay out of your head and in the conversation. This salary negotiation is just like a job interview – put your best foot forward, show confidence, be prepared to share specific examples where you demonstrated that you brought value to the company and its customers and where you demonstrated the qualities they're looking for in a candidate. Of course, not all conversations about raises are successful. Be prepared for "No," and remember, "No" isn't necessarily, "No, not ever." Ask when would be a good time to revisit the issue and follow-up. Consider too that the "No" may be the start of a conversation to discuss other compensation ideas. Perhaps a raise isn't possible now, but additional time off or other benefits can be negotiated in lieu of a salary increase.

> *Be well prepared for this conversation*
> *and your results will follow.*

Asking for the Money

One question that comes up over and over is "How do I ask for the money?"

Tim Cull, writer for the productivity blog, *LifeHacker*, shares this story about a asking for a raise:

> *"I had exhaustively researched what other developers of similar experience were making and presented it to him very methodically, building to the punch line...I'd ~~like more money please, just to, you know, be fair and~~ all.*
>
> *He stopped me in the middle, before I even got to some of the best parts that I was really proud of and said: 'Tim, why are you telling me this? You know what you should do? You need to just walk in here and say, 'I want a 15% raise' and leave it at that. I don't care what other people are making. I care about what you're making and whether or not you stay here to make it.'"*

Follow Tim's boss's advice: be confident, ask for the raise you want, believe that you're deserving. Most of all, be ready to back it up with facts describing what you've done and what you will do to earn it.

> **When asking for a raise, be prepared to tell them what you've done and what you plan to do to earn it.**

Get Engaged

Organizations that create opportunities for employees to engage with managers tend to enjoy higher retention levels and better profits as a result.

How do you get engaged? Creating a means for two-way communication leads to trust, understanding, creativity and collaboration.

When the communication is a conversation and <u>not</u> a "broadcast," both parties enjoy the experience and are truly engaged in the company. Consider this example:

> *"The director of a research department of a large advertising agency wanted to show his employees that he was approachable and open to conversation. One day he came out of his office and made a grand announcement as he walked down the hall – he said, 'OK, I'm out of my office. If anyone wants to talk to me, now is your chance.' The only thing he managed to do was to disengage us from the conversation."*
> ~Debbie Silverman

> **Create an environment where employees feel they can make a difference and where they can discuss their ideas and issues in an open forum.**

When you have an environment where people feel free to speak their mind without repercussion, you avoid disharmony and ensure harmony. For example, let's say there's an employee who puts in the required hours and more, who gets the job done, and the boss keeps piling more and more work on their plate. In an environment where people are able to speak freely, the employee could simply clarify priorities:

Boss: *"Please do this analysis and have it on my desk by the end of the week."*

Employee: *"Thanks for trusting me with this project. I'm a little concerned though that I won't be able to get it all done right and on time. Can you help me identify the most important priorities so I can concentrate on those?"*

Because the company has an open door policy, the employee is able to approach the boss, ask for guidance, and effectively complete the request.

> **Listen to your employees – they're the eyes and ears to your customers. Treat them with respect.**

You're Fired!

While this phrase is one that we've heard Donald Trump use over and over in the TV realty show, "The Apprentice," it's a phrase that causes a lot of angst to those that say it and to those that have to hear it. We'll bet your heart is pounding a little louder just by reading, "You're Fired!"

In fact, a study of human resource blogs reveals that the termination conversation is the most challenging conversation a manager can have.

If You're Being Fired

"You're Fired" shouldn't be a total shock if managers and owners are doing their jobs. If your manager or boss has had regular assessment or evaluation conversations with you, then you probably had some inkling that it was going to happen.

Let's face it: it's not a good feeling to be fired, laid off, terminated or any other lingo that means you don't work there anymore. So what should you do while this is happening and when it's over?

While you are being fired or laid off, do your best to FOCUS. Stay calm, and stay in the moment and listen to what your boss and/or HR are saying. There may be some information that will help you make the transition, such as extension of benefits and career counseling.

Even in this unhappy situation, remain professional and strive to leave on good terms. When you leave on good terms, your old employer will likely give you a good recommendation to your next employer.

> *When one door closes...consider the possibilities available rather than dwelling on the past. It's possible this is your opportunity to do something you've always wanted to do.*

When I got laid off from my six-figure sales job in the dot.com world one month after the 9-11 attacks, I wasn't sure what I should do next. I'd just moved back to South Florida after being gone for 11 years; many of my corporate contacts took financial incentive packages like I did and were retired and gone; those that weren't were hanging on to their own jobs. It was time for something different. The layoff gave me the chance to do what I do today, grow my own businesses while supporting others in growing theirs.
~Trish Carr

> *Spend your time wisely. If you want to have a pity party, allow one day and then get back to the business of marketing yourself.*

When You're Doing the Firing

When it's you doing the firing, remember to be respectful of the other person. *"To maintain perspective, picture yourself on the other side of the desk and imagine how you'd want to be treated,"* says Joanna Krotz, contributor to *Microsoft Business.*

There are thousands of blogs and articles on firing employees and most all offer the advice we give here, which is to **FOCUS:**

F: FINISH FIRST with the outcome in mind. Prepare by having a termination check list in hand.

O: OBSERVE the employee's behavior for a time and make written notes before the firing.

C: CLARIFY key employment and termination questions with HR professionals.

U: USE SPECIFIC FACTS, not emotions or personal issues when having this important conversation.

S: STAY IN THE MOMENT and do not be swayed by the employee's reaction and emotions.

Consider the following tips:

- Give good warning before firing an employee. Nothing makes an employee feel more unhappy than being blind-sided. Unless their behavior requires immediate termination, give them a fair opportunity to improve.

- Face-to-face is the considerate way to fire someone. In our technological society it isn't always possible to be "in person," but we can be face-to-face. Use video conferencing if at all possible and do not use emails, IM, voice mails or the telephone unless it's absolutely necessary.

> "When I was laid off from a middle management position at a large NY advertising agency, I learned there was something not right when my computer didn't work that day. I could turn it on but I didn't have access to the network. When I asked my boss what was going on she said she had no idea. It was after I contacted HR for someone in IT to help me that I learned that I no longer worked for the company. I was very upset by what happened and I found myself terribly disappointed in the way the company handled the layoff."
> ~Debbie Silverman

- Make sure there is a witness. Unfortunately, lawsuits happen, especially in the US where anyone can sue anybody at any time for any reason. Have a witness there, preferably someone from HR who has experience.

- Keep explanations brief. If the employee asks why they are being let go, even after you've given feedback about their performance in the past, you can say:

> "We've already discussed your performance issues. We are terminating your employment because your

performance does not meet the standards we expect at this position. We wish you well in your future endeavors and trust that you will find a position that is a better fit for you."

final. Oftentimes employees are shocked that they're being laid off and don't believe they deserve to be. Don't allow them to think that there's any chance you'll change your mind.

- Make sure the employee has no company property in their possession. Ask the employee to hand over their keys, door pass, badge, smart phone, laptop, tablet and any other company-owned equipment or supplies.

- Make sure there is no contact with the work area or coworkers. Make arrangements for them to come back at lunch or after hours to pick up their personal things. You can also arrange to send their things directly to their home. This approach will help the employee maintain dignity and will not upset other employees.

- Ensure there is no access to information systems. Before you advise the employee, remove all access to your company systems such as email, Social Media, internal networks. As noted above, make sure that the person's immediate boss and key IT people are aware of what is going on.

End the meeting on a high note or a note of empathy. The last thing we want to do is to hurt someone's self-esteem when they're being laid off. Give them details on next steps. If unemployment or continuing benefits are available to them, tell them the process and offer job search suggestions. Leave them with words of encouragement.

> *Learn more about how to better engage with your employees by stimulating the conversation at http://Consumer-Perspective.com*

Employees and Bosses and Salaries, Oh My Worksheet

Whether you are interviewing for a job or the person doing the interviewing; discussing salary and compensation, raises or job termination, remember to **FOCUS:**

F: FINISH FIRST: What is the outcome you want to achieve? Be mindful of the **Facts.**

_____

_____

_____

_____

O: OBSERVE: You can observe something about the person you are about to converse with by doing some detective work online. Check out the person or company on Google, LinkedIn and or Facebook.

Write at least three facts about the person or company that you can use to your advantage during the interview or salary conversation:

1._____

2._____

3._____

Identify at least two companies or people you can contact to pursue another job or position. Have this information available when you sense a challenge at work.

Contact #1_____

Contact #2_____

C: CLARIFY: Prepare three possible questions (or points of interest) for the interview, salary discussion or raise:

1._____

2._____

_____

3._____

_____

U: USE SPECIFIC FACTS, not emotions or personal issues when having any of these conversations.

S: STAY IN THE MOMENT: Listen to what is being said.

Download a copy of this worksheet at:
http://ItsJustaConversationBook.com/downloads

Chapter Six

Uneasy Conversations

"Houston, we have a problem."
~ Jack Swigert, Apollo 13 Astronaut

In This Chapter:
- Communication Breakdowns
- The Blame Game
- 'We Need to Talk' (Uh Oh!)
- Soft Shoe Conversation
- Out of Touch?
- Asking for the Money

Communication Breakdowns

Why do uneasy or uncomfortable conversations happen? An uneasy conversation is usually the result of one of the following breakdowns in communication:

- Someone in the conversation is rushed and distracted, thus leading the other person to feeling they're uninteresting or unimportant.

- Someone has false assumptions about something or someone.

- Someone doesn't say something or ask for clarification because they don't want to appear unintelligent; they are shy or uncomfortable asking or explaining something.

- Someone wants to be diplomatic by not bringing up a subject that might make the other person feel uncomfortable.

- Someone doesn't want to cause a fuss, and on and on.

Eventually this causes them to make assumptions that can cause havoc. And there's more:

- Someone is not listening carefully.

- Someone doesn't trust that the other person has their best interest in mind.

- Someone assumes that someone else will follow up.

- Someone doesn't allow time for the other person to ask questions.

Uneasy conversations take place in all areas of business whether you're the business owner, an employee or manager, a supplier, a 1099 contractor, a big company or a one-person business.

The scenarios we present here can be transferred to almost any interaction where people may feel uncomfortable or unsure.

Communication breakdowns can be avoided when you take the time to **FOCUS**:

F: FINISH FIRST: Consider how you want the conversation to go. **F** also stands for remain **FRIENDLY**.

O: OBSERVE AND LISTEN: If in-person, observe the other person's body language and facial expressions to see if they understand your point or request. If on the phone, listen for uncertainty. If a written conversation takes place, mind your words and don't take something out of context. Know when to stop talking and know when to listen to the person with whom you are conversing. Use the 4-Second Rule.

O also stands for **OPPORTUNITY.**

> *Instead of focusing on the challenge, focus on the person, the relationship and the opportunity.*

"Every conversation will help us learn and grow. It's not always about it being a happy conversation, but a rewarding one. And when you focus on the relationship, not the issue, the issue is magically easier to resolve," says, Karen Kimsey-House, blog author for *Huff Post Business.*

C: CLARIFY THE POINT by asking questions. If you are making the point, ask if the other person has questions about what you are saying. Let them know it's OK to ask. Instead of saying, "Do you have any questions," assume that there are questions and ask this way: "What questions do you have?" If they are making a point, ask them to clarify so they know you are genuinely interested in understanding their point.

> *When you're taking on a responsibility, always clarify that you fully understand the expectation – even if you think you already do understand, confirm it. Repeat back what you understand your responsibility to be and the expected result. Invite the other person to confirm.*

C also stands for **CALM**. Remain calm throughout the conversation. If you get excited or upset about something that is said or not said, it could turn into an unsatisfying conversation.

If you're dealing with someone who is out of control, stay calm. Barry Winbolt, psychotherapist and the author of *Difficult People*, offers the following suggestion for handling a shouter (in the context of dealing with a boss):

> *"First of all, you don't want to have the discussion mid-yell, when you're probably too flustered to make sense and the whole office may be watching. You need to find a way to postpone the conversation, by saying something like this...*

'I'd really like to talk about this. Can I come to your office in a half hour to go over the problem?' Then later, open the conversation with a line acknowledging the boss' situation, rather than putting him on the defensive."

We suggest something like this...

"I can see that work pressures are tough now and I want to help get results. I have a couple of suggestions that may make a difference for us. When it gets loud and I feel yelled at I just don't do as good a job. Can we agree that we'll keep the volume down and work together to get things done?"

C also represents **COMPROMISE** and **CONFIDENCE.**

"The goal is to develop a plan that meets the needs of your people and the business as often and as much as possible. This will usually involve a compromise; however, as long as you can find a way to give people what is most important to them, they will respect you and have confidence in your leadership," says Jessica Bunce, Office Supervisor, Department of Marketing and Department of Supply Chain Management at Michigan State University.

U: UNDERSTAND that what's being said are words that describe the situation – they don't describe you!

> *A verbal confrontation usually means that someone doesn't have all the facts. Remember, it's not personal.*

Also be sure that all parties involved in the issue have an **UNDERSTANDING** of what needs to be done and that they take the appropriate action.

Here's an example of a communication breakdown that happened because two key players did not have a good understanding of what needed to be done:

> *"As president of the Board of my association, I was talking to the manager of the building. She was concerned about a valet, who had always been a top employee, arriving at work on time or early, flexible in staying late if needed, well-liked amongst home owners and his fellow employees. The supervisor for the valets was telling the manager that this employee had become difficult, wasn't willing to change his schedule temporarily to accommodate a fellow employee's surgery and had become rude to owners and abusive to his supervisor.*
>
> *The manager was waiting for the employee to call her, which also didn't happen. I asked the manager if she had spoken to the employee directly. She had not. I recommended that she call the employee directly to set up a conversation instead of relying on the supervisor to set it up. Because the manager and supervisor were not communicating and because neither one took action to set up a conversation with the valet, the manager assumed the valet wasn't interested in talking it out and things got nasty."*
> *~Tracy Sherman, Home Owners Association President*

While the manager was waiting for a call from the employee, the employee was worried about getting fired. The supervisor told the employee that the manager wasn't happy with his performance (and that's putting it mildly), but never told him to call the manager directly. The employee thought the manager would contact him. Because of Tracy's intervention, the manager and the employee finally talked, had a productive conversation, the conflict was resolved, a valuable employee stayed and no one was fired.

S: STAY IN THE MOMENT: By staying in the moment you also demonstrate that you are a good listener.

The Blame Game

Nobody wins in the Blame Game. It often starts with someone saying something like, "You forgot to do this," or "You didn't get it to me on time," or "You misunderstood what the client needed." YOU, YOU, YOU. When you blame others for your situation or lack of success, you don't take responsibility for yourself and your actions.

Blame Game people become defensive and often lash out verbally (and sometimes physically). When that happens, things are not pretty!

Thought leader, Dr. Wayne Dyer is quoted as saying, *"All blame is a waste of time. No matter how much fault you find with another and regardless of how much you blame him, it will not change you."*

We agree! All blame is a waste of time.

How does one play the Blame Game and come out a winner? ***By looking into a mirror.***

> ***You can't change someone else. You can only change yourself.***

Take a long hard look at yourself. When you look at yourself first and analyze your actions before placing blame on someone else, chances are you'll see that there was something you could have said or done differently.

When you approach the conversation taking personal responsibility instead of an attitude of blame and frustration or anger, you'll be surprised by the cooperation and support you'll get. You also create the space for others to feel comfortable about taking responsibility for their actions.

It's not always easy to take ownership of something that didn't go right. When you find yourself blaming someone for being late in delivering a product or service, for not doing their job, for creating friction with a co-worker or for any other negative accusation, STOP! Catch yourself, take a deep breath and remember to FOCUS.

Before playing the Blame Game, ask yourself this important question: *"How much of my colleagues' performance problem did I actually own?"* says Kevin Sharer, former CEO of Amgen and current senior lecturer at Harvard Business School.

Kevin offers the following scenario that could have ended very differently if he didn't ask himself that question:

> *"The company where I served as CEO had a product and financial crisis that was playing out on the front pages of the newspapers. Our major regulator was publicly excoriating us; the stock price was plummeting. My two most capable, trusted colleagues were in charge of our day-to-day response.*
>
> *But it became apparent that, for the first time in their six year partnership – which until then had been ideal – they were not working effectively as a team. In some ways they were making things worse. My state of mind was not pretty. If you'd had a view into it, you'd have seen disgust, fury, fear and indignation."*

He asked himself the question he recommends asking, *"How much of my colleagues' performance problem did I actually own?"* and realized how he had not done his part:

> *"The following Monday, when the three of us met to review where we stood, I arrived with a different attitude. I started the meeting by describing, calmly and with total candor, how decisions I had made in the past had landed us where we were, and what I was prepared to change. In short, I owned the problem. We then decided together how we would not only manage the immediate situation but also change capabilities, priorities and processes to strengthen the company in the long run.*
>
> *I will admit that one reason my new approach allowed us to make better progress was that it stunned my colleagues. Whatever defensiveness they were feeling was swept away. But just as important, reviewing how I helped create the problem gave me more clarity and conviction about what I could fairly ask of them."*

> ***Take ownership of your part in every situation. Blame is a waste of time – even blaming yourself. Identify what you've learned and move on. There is no blame, only feedback.***

What do you do if someone is blaming you? Before you respond, take a deep breath and FOCUS. It's not personal. More often than not, the person doing the blaming is upset with themselves for something they didn't do. So don't take it personally. This, of course, is easier said than done, especially if you're on the receiving end of the YOU, YOU, YOU conversation.

The trick is to manage your mind so you don't say something you'll regret.

Here's an NLP technique that will get you through this conversation:

If you are feeling anxious, nervous, frustrated, angry, or any other negative feeling, take a deep breath and say to yourself or out loud:

"Thank you for this _____ feeling and for showing me there is an issue. I now release the root cause of this _____ feeling for my health and well-being."

Exhale and release the negative emotion you're feeling. Do this a couple of times until you feel better and are able to think rationally instead of emotionally.

> ***This exercise works for any challenging conversation and for all other times you experience these feelings.***

The Blame Game can get very uncomfortable if an ongoing problem is not addressed.

Jessica Bunce of Michigan State University suggests that to implement a solution to an ongoing issue:

"Remember to 1) Relate to the employee; 2) Ask for their input to implement a solution, and 3) Implement the solution and follow-up every time you say you will."

Jessica offers the following snippets from an actual conversation as an example:

Situation: Jane, an enraged top performer, is blaming Austin, a co-worker, for pretending to be busy typing, not doing his job and pushing the less easy tasks to her.

Jane to Bob, her manager:

"I am so frustrated with Austin. I am so irritated with his constant typing. We do the same job and I do not type half as much as he does. The typing every day is constant. Also, I always see him pull tasks out of our work queue that are easy so he can complete the same number of tasks I do, but leaves me with the time consuming and challenging international work requests. Austin's attendance is horrible and when he is here he is useless. He never greets visitors when they come in, and I think he is rude to people who call in on the phone and he is constantly asking me questions."

Bob: *"Jane, let's relax for a moment. Please have a seat and we'll talk through how we can find a solution that will work for you. So tell me more about what is truly upsetting you about Austin. If I understand you correctly you are upset with:*

- *His frequent typing*

- *Leaving you with the least easy work*

- *Austin's attendance*

- *He doesn't help you greet visitors*

- *He asks a lot of questions*

Is that correct?"

Jane: *"Yes, that covers the issues I have with him. I don't feel good about complaining, but I just want something to be done and I don't know what to do."*

Bob: *"Jane you are such an important asset to this department and you know I value your concern and want to help you. Help me find a solution that will make you happier. What would you like me to do to fix this issue and be fair to everyone, including Austin?"*

Jane: *"Well if we could, 1) share the responsibilities of greeting equally; 2) and he would try to figure out answers instead of asking so many questions; 3) share the challenging work from the queue; 4) and start working more and typing less then I would be happy. I just want to feel like he is working just as much as I am."*

Bob: *"Jane, so let's walk through this and create a plan together that we both are confident would be effective and then I will talk to Austin to make sure he does his part to improve the environment for everyone. Sound like a plan?"*

Jane: *"Yes, so what do we do?"*

Bob: *"Let's start with one issue at a time..."*

After all issues are discussed, Bob writes down an action plan and summarizes what he will do with Austin:

Bob: *"Jane, so if I implement the following action we have just written and everyone within the office agrees to do this plan, you will be satisfied with the work conditions?"*

Jane: *"Yes, absolutely."*

Bob: *"Great, so I will speak to Austin about:*

1. *Rotating the greeting;*

2. *I will be dispensing the work from the queue to be fair to everyone;*

3. *Discuss the importance of attendance; and*

4. *Schedule when Austin and I can review any challenges he is having with his work to reduce questions.*

Jane, what I ask of you is to support Austin as I work with him and try to bring him along. Treat him with kindness and be pleasant so he can experience a neutral environment while he is improving. So please be patient and help him along. Sound like a plan?"

Jane: *"Yes, I can do that."*

Bob: *"Great, thanks so much for bringing this to me and for your input."*

Because Bob was approachable and asked Jane to offer solutions to the problem and to work with Austin to bring him along, Jane was able to voice her concerns and leave Bob's office feeling like a valued and appreciated employee.

What started out as an unpleasant situation turned into a business opportunity for Bob to improve work conditions for everyone.

'We Need to Talk' (Uh Oh!)

If you have ever heard these four simple words, chances are you felt your heart beating faster and you had an uncomfortable feeling in the pit of your stomach.

"We need to talk," is a phrase you've probably heard growing up and it's important to recognize that it pushes everyone's buttons.

"When you feel your body reacting to these words, ask yourself, 'what personal history is being triggered?' You may still have the conversation, but you'll go into it knowing that some of the heightened emotional state has to do with you," says Judy Ringer, of Power & Presence Training.

As we talked about in the Blame Game section, use the same NLP technique to change your thinking about having a "We Need to Talk" conversation:

If you are feeling intimidated, belittled, ignored, frustrated, angry, or any other negative feeling, take a deep breath and then say to yourself or out loud:

"Thank you for this _____ feeling and for showing me there is an issue. I now release the root cause of this _____ feeling for my health and well-being."

Exhale and release the negative emotion you're feeling. Do this a couple of times until you feel better and are able to think rationally instead of emotionally.

> *Pay close attention to the 'root cause' of the feeling. You probably didn't even know that there was something else that initiated this negative reaction.*

Oftentimes when we hear, "We need to talk," we make assumptions about the other person's intentions. *"You may feel intimidated, belittled, ignored, disrespected or marginalized, but be cautious about assuming that that was their intention.* **Impact does not necessarily equal intent**," says Judy Ringer.

Judy goes on to say, *"'We need to talk' often triggers your mind to wander into a myriad of 'what if' scenarios, most often into the worst case scenarios. Stay present and in the moment so your thoughts don't escalate into unnecessary anxiety."*

To get through a "We need to talk" conversation, consider the following:

1. Adjust your attitude for maximum effectiveness. Use one of the NLP techniques offered – see the NLP technique above and in Chapter Three on page 48.

2. Cultivate an approach of discovery and curiosity. Learn as much as you can from the other person by listening for what is said and not said, and watch their body language.

3. Acknowledge whatever you can to show that you've heard and understood what the other person is saying to you. They won't change unless they see that you see where they stand.

> *If you are the boss and you must have a strong conversation with an employee, don't say, 'We need to talk!' You're pushing buttons unnecessarily.*

127

As a follow-up to the conversation between Bob and Jane in The Blame Game section, Austin was asked to go into Bob's office. Here's how that conversation went:

Bob: *"Austin, I wanted to discuss a few things and I'd like to start by finding out about how everything is going for you here. Tell me what you think about your work environment."*

Notice that Bob did not use a threatening tone and that he did not say, "We need to talk." He started by asking an open-ended question about Austin's perception of the work environment.

He didn't label anything or say anything negative about his performance. He made no judgments and kept an open mind. He asked an open-ended question to solicit information.

Austin provided a lot of information to Bob including that he didn't know how to handle international clients – which was why he didn't do it and pushed it on to Jane.

Bob: *"Austin, I want you to know that improving the environment for you is very important to me. If I had some suggestions straight from your peers on what you could do to be truly accepted as part of a team, would you take action?"*

Austin: *"Yes, I will do almost anything at this point just to feel better when I come to work."*

Because of Bob's approach, Austin felt more at ease and could freely express his concerns. Also, Bob's considerate approach allowed Austin to save face and to be creative in his own right with how he could help turn things around.

If Bob had said, "We need to talk," there's a very good chance that Austin would have become defensive and would have blamed Jane and others for his shortcomings.

In addition to the way Bob handled the conversation, consider the following conversation openers from Judy Ringer:

"I have something I'd like to discuss with you that I think will help us work together more effectively.

I'd like to talk with you about _____, and first I'd like to get your point of view.

I need your help with what just happened. Do you have a few minutes to talk?" (We personally use the "I need your help" statement a lot – especially when dealing with slow moving companies and employees.)

"I need your help with something. Can we talk about it soon?" If they say, *"Sure, let me get back to you,"* make sure to follow up.

"I think we have different perceptions about _____. I'd like to hear your thinking on this."

"I'd like to talk about ____. I think we may have different ideas on how to _____."

"I'd like to see if we might reach a better understanding about _____. I really want to hear your feelings about this and share my perspective as well."

Soft Shoe Conversation

What is a soft shoe conversation?

A soft shoe conversation is when you take a soft approach in a challenging situation or one where you want to tell someone "No," in a diplomatic way.

A soft shoe conversation, when managed correctly, ends without anyone feeling hurt or creating another uneasy conversation. The key to success is being straight forward and diplomatic.

In a soft shoe conversation you keep your voice, body language and facial expressions free and easy.

Here's an example of how to say "No" to someone using the soft shoe approach:

"I asked a relative of mine that held a senior level position at a very large company to provide some conversation examples for this book. He said, 'Thanks for your offer to make a contribution, but I have nothing to offer. The 'conversations' that pass through my memory are trivial and dull. Good luck."

~Debbie Silverman

> **When you want to say, "No," keep it short and make it about you, not the other person.**

How do you say "No" to your boss?

"Anytime I've had to say 'No' to a boss, they've always appreciated it. And I know as a boss myself, I'd much rather you be honest with me than take the chance you

won't be able to do what I asked. I don't like surprises.
Tell me right away that there might be a challenge and
what you think the solution is and I'll respect you for it."
     ~Trish Carr

Prepare saying "No" to your boss by remembering to
FOCUS:

F: FINISH FIRST: Begin with the outcome in mind —
prepare your talking points in advance of the meeting and
practice saying them out loud.

O: OPEN THE CONVERSATION with an appreciation for
your manager's confidence in you.

C: CLEARLY STATE THE REASON why you think you may
not be able to take on additional work, or whatever you are
saying "No" to. "I'd love to and at this time it doesn't work for
me because..."

U: USE SPECIFIC FACTS: Keep emotions or personal
issues out when having this important conversation.

S: STAY IN THE MOMENT and do not be swayed by your
boss' reaction and emotions. If the manager is good they'll
match and mirror your tone and behavior so that you won't
feel uncomfortable.

"Learning how to say 'No' to your boss the right way is
essential in demonstrating your ability to effectively
manage work and make decisions based on priorities. If
you take on too much and can't get it done, or worse, play

> *the martyr, take it on and complain the whole time,*
> *you're not showing the kind of attitude and leadership*
> *that employers want and reward."*
> ~Trish Carr

Out of Touch?

So, you want to call a business associate or client you haven't spoken with in a while.

For some, this can be a daunting conversation if you allow yourself to think that way.

Instead, consider this, what if the person you want to call, and haven't spoken to in six months or longer is thinking about you and doesn't have the time to look up your contact information? Or, what if they are embarrassed to call you too? What if your product or service could be just what they need right now?

What happens if you don't make that call or email that person? NOTHING! Nothing happens for you, for your company or for them. The opportunity to continue the relationship and/or make a sale may go to someone else.

Don't let the passage of time be the reason a connection or client gets away. Changing that thinking and being prepared with what to say and how to say it makes it easier to make those calls and send those emails.

So how do you get back in touch? What do you say?

1. Acknowledge that it's been a while. A few ways to address it are:

   • *"It's been too long since we talked. I think of you often and this time I finally said to myself, stop what you're doing, pick up the phone and give her a call."*

- *"It's so great to hear your voice. I'm sure you're surprised to hear from me after so long. When was the last time we spoke? Could it be when you got promoted last year?"*

- *"I trust you're doing well. I apologize for not being in touch sooner. I've had a full schedule that keeps me so busy. I know you probably do too. I've missed keeping in touch with you."*

2. Explain the reason for your call. You may want to reconnect for any number of reasons or simply for the sake of keeping the relationship going. Whatever the reason, don't hide it or dance around it.

   - *"I thought of you because I'm considering a job change and wanted to ask your opinion on how best to find the right thing?*

   - *A few months ago you told me you wanted a way to lose weight. We have a new product that's getting rave reviews and incredible results. I'd love to show it to you."*

> **When contacting someone after it's been awhile, reach out through Social Media and reconnect before the phone call. Assume they'd love to hear from you. They were busy too.**

Asking for the Money

While some business owners have the confidence to set their pricing and get what they ask for, others question themselves and don't ask for their worth – they're reluctant to ask clients to pay up.

Why do we dance around the subject when it comes to asking for money?

- Do we think that if we have to ask, the client isn't happy with our services or products?

- Do we question our self-worth?

- Do we think that perhaps they won't like us if we ask to get paid?

- What is there to fear?

If you are in business, there's a very good chance you are selling something — either your services or a product.

Successful business people must be comfortable asking to be paid. Inventor of the Infomercial, original Shark on ABC TV's *Shark Tank*, and *As Seen On TV* pioneer, Kevin Harrington offers these words of advice to anyone concerned with asking for the sale:

"When you're nervous about asking for the sale, think about how much better that person's life is going to be after buying your product or service. You're solving a problem with what you're selling, you're improving their life and giving them a better solution to an issue that they're having. Make sure they can benefit by it and then be confident in the fact that you're making a difference in their life."

Just like asking for a raise, asking to get paid is about **FOCUS:**

F: FINISH FIRST: Keep in mind, the outcome is to get paid for providing your product or service. Know your value and recognize that asking to get paid completes your obligation to your customer and theirs to you.

O: OBSERVE AND LISTEN to your client. They may be going through a challenging time and need extra time to pay.

"By engaging your client in a conversation about paying up, you might be able to find a way to agree on terms that help them better run their business," says S. Anthony Iannarino in his blog, *Asking Your Clients to Pay Up.*

C: CLARIFY THE ISSUE around payment and be **CREATIVE**. Offer your client a way to pay you that suits both parties. You can bill them in increments (half down when they sign the agreement and the balance when the product or service is delivered); give them 60-day terms and bill the client's credit card on the first day of the billing cycle. This will give the client more time.

> *"When signing up for a high value marketing program, I asked if they would work with me on a payment schedule. The company that was offering this program was set in their ways about the payment. I had to pay in full or I didn't get the program. A colleague suggested that I find a credit card that offered 0% interest for 6 months or a year. This was a terrific idea and made the payments a lot easier."*
> ~Debbie Silverman

U: USE YOUR EXPERIENCE and success to take the fear out of asking for your money. Remind yourself that you've been compensated for your talents in the past and this is no different.

S: STAY IN THE MOMENT: Ask for what you want. When you find yourself in your head, bring yourself back to the moment.

When asking for money, keep the following in mind:

> ***Be polite, professional and direct.***

"One fast way to make an uncomfortable conversation even more uncomfortable is to dance around the subject," says Tim Cull, *LifeHacker* blogger. *"Say, 'I'm raising my rates,' and give a brief explanation why. You may want to say something like, 'I haven't raised my rates in 3 years and I'm raising my rates by $___ or___ %.'"*

> ***Ask for what you want.***

Yes, do your homework and find out the going rate. Use that information for your pricing. However, don't compare yourself to others when asking for your price; you are unique and offer value no one else does, because they're buying YOU!

In her book, *Put More Cash in Your Pocket*, Loral Langemeier, money expert and 5-time NY Times and Wall Street Journal bestselling author says, *"Powerful words are always helpful. Sentences such as, 'When do you want me to*

start?' and, 'How would you like to pay?' create an assumption*
that the deal is going to close."

When you're asking for business Loral suggests this direct approach:

"I'm the owner of All Natural Cleaners. I'd like to make
your home healthy as well as spotless. I can schedule you for
a day next week. Would Thursday work?"

Be direct, be confident and know that what you're offering provides real value. You're making a difference, you're solving challenges and you're making life easier, so expect to be paid in return.

You agreed on a price, you delivered a product or service; you've followed up with invoices and statements and still haven't gotten paid. Here's an example of what to say when a customer is a late payer:

"Bob, the invoices from May and June are overdue. Would it
be better if I came by Tuesday or Friday to pick up a check?"

Notice there is no judgment in this language; you're being firm, offering options and stating confidently what you want.

Uneasy Conversations Worksheet

Have to say "No" to a boss? Find yourself blaming someone else for an issue? Want to connect with a client with whom you lost touch? Take a deep breath and **FOCUS:**

F: FINISH FIRST: What is the outcome you want to achieve? Be mindful of the **facts**.

_____

_____

_____

_____

O: OBSERVE: You can observe something about the person you are about to converse with by doing some detective work online. Check out the person or company on Google, LinkedIn and or Facebook.

Write down at least three facts about the person or company that you can use to your advantage during the challenging conversation.

1._____

2._____

3._____

C: CLARIFY: Prepare three possible questions or points of interest for the conversation. If you are the boss, prepare three questions you could use to get the employee to create the solution:

1._____

_____

2._____

_____

3._____

_____

U: USE SPECIFIC FACTS, not emotions or personal issues when having any of these conversations. Also, jot down two or three reasons you can't make the commitment or why you have to say 'No.' A good statement that works is, "It doesn't work for me, what I can do is…." Whenever you can, follow up your no with an alternative solution.

1._____

2._____

3._____

S: STAY IN THE MOMENT and listen to what is being said. Practice listening to people as though you had to repeat all their words.

Download a copy of this worksheet at:
http://ItsJustaConversationBook.com/downloads

Chapter Seven

The New Networking – Creating Relationships Not Just Leads

"The richest people in the world look for and build networks, everyone else just looks for work."
~Robert Kiyosaki, author, "Rich Dad Poor Dad"

In This Chapter:
- Why Network?
- Networking Do's & Don'ts
- Think Before You Speak
- How Do I Start?
- Take it Up a Notch

It surprises us how many people don't do any networking at all. Even more surprising is how many people attend networking events, make connections and then do nothing with them. Networking is a vital component to continuous growth, for your business and for yourself. You may be the best in your field, but eventually you'll have to add new prospects and new customers with whom to share your products and services. It's been said that everything we want in life comes through other people and that being the case, doesn't it make sense that we'd want to meet lots and lots of them?

> *Networking and relationship building are essential to success in businesses and in life.*

Why Network?

- The more people you meet, the more referrals you get.

- Discover new ways to get business.

- Identify potential clients or customers.

- Talking to people helps you generate new ideas.

- Find new strategic partners, create joint ventures.

- Find new products and services you need.

- Repeating and practicing your elevator speech makes you a better communicator.

- Meet mentors and coaches who can accelerate your results.

- Mix and mingle with like-minded people and create new areas of business and new friendships.

Networking Do's & Don'ts

While we're surprised that some business people don't network and don't follow up, what's even more surprising is that many don't know the basics of networking. Too often you'll be approached by someone solely focused on telling you how great their product or service is. They give you their canned speech about their product, and all the while you're just looking for a way out rather than a way in. We're sure you can relate to being in one of these conversations. We've all been accosted by the salesperson who says the same thing to everyone, who does all the talking, who is old school, high pressure sales.

Do...

- Make it a conversation rather than a monologue.

- Sound authentic.

- Stay attentive.

- Talk to and about them.

- Stay on point, be succinct.

One networking faux pas is handing your business card to someone in response to, "What do you do?" Networking is meant to bring two people together, not two business cards. We're reminded of what we hear moms say to their toddlers, "Use your words, honey." Your business card in my face could say that your communication skills may not be that great, that you're shy, that you may be unsure of yourself, or any number of things that aren't necessarily good.

So, what should you do when networking? **FOCUS:**

F: FINISH FIRST: Consider your intended outcomes - how many contacts do you want to make? Who do you want to meet? Go in with the idea that there are two or three people who really want to meet **you**.

O: OPEN UP and get out of your comfort zone.

C: CONNECT with people in a way that shows you really want to get to know them, stay **CALM** and be **CONFIDENT.**

U: BE UNIQUE

S: STAY IN THE MOMENT: Stay out of your head and in the conversation.
   Easy ways to display confidence and be relatable:

- Smile!

- Introduce yourself with your first **and** last name.

- Focus on the other person.

- Let them do most of the talking.

- Ask open-ended questions.

- Connect them with other people.

- Be interested, not interesting.

- Listen actively, nod, react, show interest.

- Search for common ground.

> **When you carry yourself with confidence and focus on the other person, you open up the relationship.**

Remember to use the Rules of Etiquette in Chapter One:

Think Before You Speak

Know something about the person (or reason that brought you together) – in this case, you're both there to build relationships.

- Remember and use their name.

- Stick with Safe Topics.

- Remember the need for reciprocity – conversation is give and take.

- Listen!

How Do I Start?

Keep your conversation starters simple and relatable. Here are a few easy openers:

At the buffet table:

> *"Yum, have you ever tried these?"*
> *"I wonder what that is. Do you know?"*
> *"It's great that there are so many healthy choices. What looks good to you?"*

Connect with someone standing or sitting on their own:

> *"Wow, there are so many people here. It's a little noisy (or crazy, or loud, or high energy). Is it OK if I join you over here where it's quieter?"*
>
> *"Sometimes there are so many people at these events that I don't know where to start. May I join you?"*

Compliment them:

> *"Oh that drink looks refreshing. What is it?"*
> *"That's a bold tie, I like it. You have good taste."*
> *"Now that's a welcoming smile…"*

Talk About Sports:

If you're a sports person, use your knowledge to your advantage. If you see someone wearing team memorabilia, or hear people having sports conversations, use it as your opening:

> *"Oh, I see you're a fan of Big Blue. How'd you end up a Michigan fan?"*

(On overhearing a group talking about sports…) *"Are you talking about…? Yes, that was an incredible play, wasn't it?"*

Just Say Hello:

Oftentimes the easiest way to break the ice is to simply offer a confident handshake and smile, and say,
> *"Hi, I'm _____."*

Keep the conversation moving. An easy next thing to talk about is something you obviously have in common – you're both attending this event!

Ask about attending this event:

"First time at this event?"
"How'd you hear about this event?"
"This is a good location for this event. Have you ever been here before?"

Learn more about them:

"Do you live nearby?"
"Tell me about your family?"
"Where did you grow up?"
"What made you move here?"
"Tell me more about your business."
"What do you like about living there?"

> **Keep your conversations positive. If something at the event is not going well, e.g., it's too hot, the food isn't good, it's crowded and loud; do not dwell on those as a way to gain rapport. You'll soon find yourself in a negative spiral that could lead you down a negative path.**

"I was at an event where a lot of people were complaining about everyone tripping on the carpet. The conversation

about it continued on so long you could actually feel the energy in the room go down. I made a request that we focus on the swift action by the staff and move on to learning more about each other. We did and the energy shift was immediate, allowing for a much more rewarding experience for everyone."

~ Trish Carr

> **Let the conversation flow, listen and build rapport by listening for commonalities, possibilities and opportunities to add value, to support them, to take the relationship to the next level.**

Take it Up a Notch

Bob Burg, author of *The Go-Giver*, speaker and creator of the business building, *Endless Referrals* system says, *"All things being equal, people will do business with, and refer business to, those people they know, like and trust."*

That being the case, doesn't it make sense that we want people to feel good around us and to like us? Wouldn't we always want to put our best foot forward, make a good impression, and leave people feeling good about us and our conversation?

The best way for people to feel good about you is to help them feel good about *themselves*, and the most natural way to do that, is to have an interest in them. In his article, *How to Cultivate a Network of Endless Referrals & Develop Profitable, Win/Win Relationships,* Bob Burg suggests the following "Feel Good" networking questions:

"How did you get started in the 'widget' business?" Bob says, *"I call this the 'Movie-of-the-Week' question because most people love the opportunity to 'tell their story' to someone. This, in a world where most people don't care enough to want to know their story."*

"What do you enjoy most about what you do?" Bob explains, *"Again, you are giving them something very positive to associate with you and your conversation. You are making them feel special, important."*

Networking is just a conversation. The more you do it, the better your conversations get. Get out there. Get in the game. And then...

"Treat each person you meet as if they are 'The One."
~Nancy Matthews, Author of The One Philosophy

The One Philosophy means treating *every* person you meet with the same level of attention and respect as you would the person you *knew* was The One.

Building relationships means getting to know people letting them get to know the authentic you, understanding who they are, their point of view and their values.

> *Go beyond the usual chatter and you'll create relationships that are fast, deep and meaningful.*

Ask open-ended questions, find out about what motivates them, about their family, their experiences, their life. Have a conversation; ask questions that give insight into who they are and what's important to them. Listen intently focusing on them. From there it's easy to build a real relationship, one that serves you both inside your work and inside your life.

When we meet people at events or in our everyday life, so often we are coming from our own agenda, looking for how that person might be able to help us, how we might do business together, "What's in it for me?"

Duane Cummings does exactly the opposite. You remember Duane's story about getting past the gatekeeper? He was the one who found out he was courting the owner's mother, not just the receptionist, and landed his largest account because he didn't look past her.

When Duane meets someone and makes a connection, he sets out to make a difference in that person's life. He doesn't know how or when, he just knows that at some point, he'll do something that'll make a positive difference. He doesn't look for what's in it for him, he doesn't keep score.

> *Change your networking focus from, "What do you do?" to, "What can I do for you?"*

Duane's story below illustrates the magic that can happen when you leave your agenda behind, value others and remember, *It's Just a Conversation...*

"A couple years ago I was flying home and sitting right beside me is the defensive coordinator for the college football team in my home town."

You could hear Duane light up as he talked about it. He's a big sports guy and his team is a perennial nationally-ranked contender.

"So, you have a couple options," he said. You could say, "Hi, nice to meet you," or, as I would normally do, and with it I did, I engaged him, and we talked for two hours. About everything from being a coach and what your passion and mission is, to talking about his wife's passing and how that affected him, his team, etc."

Even if you're not a football fan, there's probably a lot to learn from a man who produces winners year after year. What did Duane do, what did he say to *engage* the football coach and take the conversation to the next level?

"I let him know that I was a coach too, and I asked him about the challenges that he faced. I told him quickly my story about leaving coaching. I talked about the demands it puts on your family and what that cost might be."

Now at this point, you might be asking, "It's all well and good that Duane met the coach, but how does all this relate to doing business?" Here's the lesson Duane shared:

"In reality, if you begin to build a rapport with someone, you can change gears faster than other people might. So, where it might take somebody three meetings to get to where they should be, I usually get there in one."

You never know what can happen once you open a relationship with the intention of listening and adding value.

When you come from the intention of making a difference for others, things line up in your favor. Duane knows this firsthand. As a result of connecting with the coach:

"Subsequently, I've taken the executive leadership team from the company I'm working with now to the University and we did a leadership day with the coaches."

Duane's ability to build rapport and comfortably and naturally open a relationship during a chance meeting made it possible for him to get a foot in the door of a world-renowned university, WOW his client by taking him there and learn from a top-notch team of leaders.

It kept getting better,

"And last week I'm coming back from Houston and one of his assistant coaches, who I hadn't met yet, is getting on my plane. We had a conversation and, as it turns out, the assistant coach's middle son has a passion for soccer. We have season tickets so now he and his family are going to come with us."

Wonderful — a personal connection, too. But wait, there's more:

"And then that conversation led to him saying he's having challenges inspiring some of his players beyond thinking about just today, about leaving a legacy and giving them purpose. So he wants me to come and speak to those players. And that all started because the defensive coordinator got on a plane and I spoke to him. And now, there's this deeper connection to an organization, to the

people, and it's not about how can I wiggle my way in there, it's just about fulfilling your purpose."

We invite you to *Take it Up a Notch*, show interest in people, build rapport, be open to possibilities, throw out the agenda and make a difference.

"Every relationship begins as a seed of possibility for something great to grow." ~Trish Carr

The New Networking - Creating Relationships Not Just Leads Worksheet

Remember, the goal is to open a relationship. **FOCUS:**

F: FEEL GOOD QUESTIONS are a great way to build rapport. Consider using these questions from Bob Burg:
"How did you get started in the 'widget' business?"
"What do you enjoy most about what you do?"

O: OPENING THE CONVERSATION: Consider your opening statement or question.
Write down three or more ways you can open a conversation:

1._____
_____
2._____
_____
3._____
_____

C: CLARIFY: How do you answer the question, "What do you do?"

_____
_____
_____

U: UNIQUE: What's different about you? What makes your business, product and/or service unique? Write down three or more ways your business is unique:

1._____
2._____
3._____

S: STAY IN THE MOMENT: Give the gift of your presence. Write down three ways you can be a better listener.

1._____
2._____
3._____

Download a copy of this worksheet at:
http://ItsJustaConversationBook.com/downloads

Chapter Eight

Leadership Conversations for the 21st Century

"A leader takes people where they want to go. A great leader takes people where they don't necessarily want to go, but ought to be."
~Rosalynn Carter, Former First Lady

In This Chapter:
- It's an Inside Job
- Inspiring for Performance
- One Size Does NOT Fit All

It's an Inside Job

Let's start with making an important distinction. The terms "Leader" and "Manager" are often used inter-changeably. Effective leaders possess the qualities of managers in terms of "managing" the business:

157

- Focusing people on producing specific results

- Budgeting for efficiency in reaching those results

- Getting things done

- Measuring results

- Clearing challenges

- Strategizing, planning and implementing

- Influencing others to get the job done

There are probably a few more you can think of too. A good manager can do all the things listed above. The distinction is that leaders possess the additional characteristic of *bringing out the best and, oftentimes, the extraordinary in people.* This trait, this quality is inherent in great leaders.

A manager can get the work done. A manager can move the numbers in the right direction, but a leader inspires people beyond their existing thinking and behavior to grow and expand, thereby expanding the company, the project, the community, and the people involved.

Leadership is the ability to tap into people's greatness and inspiring them to achieve for themselves rather than for their paycheck or for your cause. Leaders have the skill to inspire others, to uncover their passion and ignite their intrinsic need to be a part of something bigger, to contribute, to seek fulfillment.

The most successful leaders know how to **FOCUS:**

F: FINISH FIRST: Successful leaders have a plan in mind, a plan for a common vision for the organization.

O: OBSERVE AND LISTEN to others. Great leaders don't focus on themselves, they focus on others.

C: CLARIFY points by asking questions to make sure everyone is on the same page.

U: BE UNIQUE and be yourself. And, match and mirror (the best you can) to create rapport. **U** also stands for **UNDERSTAND.** Effective leaders understand the needs of the people involved and use this understanding to inspire performance.

S: STAY IN THE MOMENT: Strong leaders stay in the moment, listen and see all sides of a situation.

> *Leaders are inspiring rather than directive.*

We say that leadership is an inside job because it's more about uncovering and stirring something inside people than it is about "telling" people what to do.

You cannot be a great leader if the focus is on you. Great leaders understand that the focus must be on others first and foremost.

On adding value to the world through people, trusted leadership authority and best-selling author, John Maxwell says, *"To add value to others, you must first **value** others."*

This is the first commandment of a great leader.

"People before profits. Since everything, including profits, comes through other people, when you focus on people first, you're starting on the piece that matters most."
~ *Nancy Matthews, CEO WPNGlobal.com*

Inspiring for Performance

"Great leaders focus on creating a common vision and inspiring people to contribute to that vision."
~Trish Carr

If you're a boss you may be thinking, *"Yes, I love people; yes, I get it that great leaders inspire rather than command. But let's talk about reality! Some people just can't be inspired and the work has to get done."*

We can relate to that! Most of us regularly deal with under-performing employees, partners, co-workers, leaders, supervisors and team members, all of whom can gum up the works and slow down achieving the intended result.

Yes, we do need to get the job done, but at what cost? You can go back to the old way of managing by objectives and/or managing by fear, but to make the difference only a leader can make, to inspire people to take it on, to make it their own, to give it their best, you've got to do more than give orders.

When you inspire people in this way, you make an investment in them. Your time now helps them do it right the next time and the time after that, thereby reducing the time needed from you in the long run. And isn't that the ultimate goal? To create leaders who can expand the mission of your enterprise whether it be your budding start-up, your community project or your multi-national corporation.

Let's put this philosophy into words. Take a look at the conversations below to illustrate the point.

Boss: *"Chris, we're a week away from deadline and you still haven't turned in your outline on the project.*

Chris: *"Sorry boss, I'm working on it. I got backed up because..."*

Boss: *"I don't need excuses. If I don't have it on my desk before 5PM today you're off the team."*

It's unfortunate to say we hear some version of this more often than we'd like. Sometimes it's not easy to keep your cool when people let you down, it's not easy when you're responsible for results and the people you manage or your team members aren't getting their end done. In this case, Chris' boss is obviously feeling pressure.

> ### *Let people have their say.*

When the boss interrupts and doesn't allow Chris the opportunity to explain the situation, it shuts Chris down. That one interaction can make the difference between Chris feeling valued and Chris feeling disrespected and disengaged from the conversation.

As the manager or boss, you can threaten, cajole and order the team member to do what you want and you may get the result you're seeking. However, this approach may create stress and lead to an even more challenging conversation down the road.

In his book, *Jack: Straight from the Gut*, legendary CEO and business leader, Jack Welch, outlined this theory on the performance of individual contributors:

> 10% of people are low performers
> 70% want to do a good job and are trainable
> 20% are top performers.

Let's assume that Chris is in the 70% and is someone who usually gets the job done but may need some coaching along the way. This might be a better way to handle the same conversation with the same outcome for the business objective AND a favorable outcome for Chris:

Boss: *"Chris, the outlines for the project are due and I didn't receive yours yet. What's happening?"*

Chris: *"Sorry about that boss. I should've told you I was waiting to hear back from Margie in accounting with the final numbers."*

> ### *Remember the 4-Second Rule...*

Chris: *"They just reached my desk, I'm working on the final outline and I'll have it to you within the hour."*

This conversation had a totally different outcome when it comes to Chris' *future* motivation. This time, the boss didn't interrupt. She heard Chris out. She showed respect and confidence in Chris. She withheld judgment and kept the relationship whole.

> *A good manager gets results, a great manager gets results and keeps the relationship whole.*

Now let's take the conversation to the next level, to the leadership level:

Boss: *"Thanks for your outline Chris. (Wait 4 seconds.) Good job including all the major points. I especially appreciate the extra effort in getting the most recent numbers from Margie. That was a good idea."*

> ***Start coaching by focusing on what's right.***

Chris: *"Thank you. Margie actually suggested it. I'm sorry that waiting for it made me late."*

Boss: *"Apology accepted. I imagine you were concerned when you didn't have it in time."*

> ***Empathize and relate as to how they may have felt. Open up the relationship and build trust.***

Boss: *"What happened?"*

Chris: *"Margie just fell behind and didn't tell me she wasn't going to make my deadline until it was too late."*

(Wait 4 seconds...)

Boss: *"How'd you find out?"*

Chris: *"When I didn't have them by 3:00, I sent an email. When she still hadn't gotten back to me by 4, I called and left a voice mail and I sent a text. I figured I'd try all three. But by then I was already overdue in getting it to you."*

(Wait 4 seconds...)

Chris: *"I probably should've told you before you had to ask me."*

(Wait 4 seconds...)

Boss: *"That probably would've been a good idea. What difference might it have made if you let me know sooner?"*

Chris: *"You may have told me to ditch getting the figures or you may have told me it was OK to wait another couple of hours. Of course that's not true, but I think if I told you sooner, I would've at least known what you thought."*

(Wait 4 seconds...)

Chris: *"Yeah, I should've let you know rather than be late."*

Boss: *"Yes, it might've given me a chance to support you in getting what you needed. It would have been easier if you'd just let me know. Chris, what will you do differently next time?"*

> **Instead of "telling" how they should be done it, ask questions so they can uncover the answers themselves.**

Once you open up the conversation, listen to hear what happened. Continue the conversation asking questions to guide them to creating their own answers and seeing their responsibility in the situation.

Chris had many ways to deal with the situation sooner. Knowing when to ask for help and actually asking for it is another quality of leadership.

Having this conversation with Chris will not only help Chris be a better performer day-to-day, it will also help him to eventually outgrow his current position. And isn't that what we really want, to see Chris excel? Great leaders create great leaders.

Great leaders get personal satisfaction helping others be the best they can be.

> **Great leaders view missteps as opportunities for growth and as opportunities to serve. Great leaders ask, "How can I support this person so that they are better because of this experience?"**

*"Great leaders build great people, and great
people build great businesses."*
~Trish Carr

> **When you inspire people to a higher level
> and create opportunity for their growth,
> you make a difference in their future and
> you move yourself from a great manager
> to a great leader.**

One Size Does NOT Fit All

*"I know there is strength in the differences between us. I
know there is comfort where we overlap."*
~Ani DiFranco, poet, singer, songwriter

Leaders understand that while there are many commonalities among people, we all have different personalities, different styles of communicating and different approaches to life. Great leaders adjust their style to fit the person and situation, rather than expecting the person to adjust to the leader. This is the epitome of matching and mirroring that has been discussed throughout this book.

Why is an employee's communication style important to understand?

*"If you want to make yourself understood easily and
quickly, you need to address someone using his or her
dominant system for processing information. People
simply do not find it easy to make sense of or relate to*

language that is not in their representational style," says, Dr. Yvonne Oswald, author of *Every Word Has Power.*

To match and mirror successfully, it is important to recognize the four representational systems people use to process information. *"A good way to remember is look, listen, think or feel," says Dr. Oswald.*

Visual – They tend to talk quickly, have a higher-pitched voice, are less distracted by noise and will respond to visual language such as "look" or "see."

Auditory – Their voice usually has more tonality (a bit like a radio announcer). They enjoy talking on the phone, they like music and are more easily distracted by noise.

Auditory-digital –These are the people that self-talk. It has to be logical and make sense to these people for it to be understood. They think in sequences and like a step-by-step process.

Kinesthetic – They usually "feel" life by trusting with their gut instinct or feeling. They usually speak with slower, deliberate phrasing and use longer, more complex sentences.

Here's a terrific example of recognizing and matching communication styles:

"For almost 30 years I was a manager of 8-12 supervisors – both in Engineering and Operations. It really didn't matter what our 'jobs' were so much as how we interacted with each other. Having so many different personalities on my

team made it very difficult to get everybody on the same page at the same time. Fortunately, my employer saw the benefit in providing leadership training to all second level managers.

It was during one such course that I learned the most valuable lesson in leadership and one that I still use today with everyone I encounter. The course's basic premise was that 'one size does not fit all.' The lesson learned and applied was that in order to be the most effective leader, I needed to adapt my personality to that of my team member. This meant that I shouldn't approach every person the same way and that my behavior needed to change depending on the type of person I was talking to.

For example, one of my supervisors had a very strong Type A (driver) personality. I learned that when I came into her cubicle in the morning, that I didn't need to discuss her commute, the weather or her kids. I needed to get right down to business and do it quickly and then leave.

On the other hand, Connie, another supervisor, was a social extrovert which meant I did need to take time to chat about the non-business items before getting to the business issues.

Then there was Pam, the analytic, who I had to be prepared with facts and stats when approaching her with any business idea. The course taught us how to identify everyone's style and the best communication style to use with each. I found it extremely valuable in being able to "reach" each one of my team members to gain their trust and cooperation.

~Diane Delgouffre, Project Manager
Osmose Communications, Contractor for AT&T

Diane's story clearly illustrates the importance of understanding other people's communication styles so that your conversations create the outcome you want.

> *If you approach a CPA the same way you approach a party planner, you'll likely get two different outcomes. People are different and the differences are what make teams work. Great leaders know how to adjust their style to communicate with maximum influence.*

Listen for clues, pay attention to how you're approached. Match and mirror.

> *Learn more about identifying and maximizing communication styles to accelerate your business at http://TrishCarr.com*

Leadership Conversations for the 21st Century Worksheet

Remember, leadership is about inspiring people to be and to do their best. Make the most of your performance improvement conversations with **FOCUS**:

F: FINISH FIRST: As a leader, what is the outcome you want to achieve?

_____

_____

_____

_____

O: OBSERVE AND LISTEN to others. Practice observing others and identifying their communication style.
Write down your style and how it compares to theirs:

1._____
2._____
3._____

C: CLARIFY: Prepare three questions before you have your conversation:

1._____
2._____
3._____

U: BE UNIQUE in your style and shape it to match and mirror the person you're talking with so that they feel comfortable.

S: STAY IN THE MOMENT: You can practice staying in the moment before you get to the conversation. Remember and practice this simple exercise to stay in the moment: Think of a person, place or thing. Really focus on that particular thought. Now let your mind wander to another person, place or thing. When you feel your mind shifting to another thought, say to yourself, "stay in the moment" and take your mind back to the original thought. It takes some practice. You will notice in a short time that you are more focused and more in the moment.

Download a copy of this worksheet at:
http://ItsJustaConversationBook.com/downloads

Just One More Quick Conversation

"I really didn't say everything I said."
~Yogi Berra, baseball legend, known for pithy quotes

No matter the subject, everything in business and in life is *Just a Conversation*. Anything can be accomplished when people communicate in the spirit of collaboration and win-win.

Effective communication is of course all about **FOCUS**:

F: FINISH FIRST: set your intention for the outcome before you start.

O: OBSERVE: Look and listen closely to the person you are talking to.

C: CLARIFY: Ask questions and remain **CALM.**

U: UNIQUE: Be true to yourself.

S: STAY IN THE MOMENT: Stay out of your head and in the conversation.

Be aware that your conversation starts before any words are spoken. Whether your conversation is in person, by phone, email or Social Media, remember that your body language, voice tone and facial expressions speak volumes.

Use silence - the 4-Second Rule for usual conversations, and the 10-Second Rule when negotiating. Silence helps you control the conversation and your thoughts. It also shows that you are listening.

Remember Pat and Chris' conversation in the Introduction of the book? Here's what happened the first time:

"Hi Chris, this is Pat, how are you?"

"Hi Pat, I've been better. I'm putting out a fire here at the office."

"OK, I just need a minute of your time. My company just came out with an amazing breakthrough product that would be perfect for you and your company."

"Well it doesn't matter if it's better than oxygen. I'm up to my elbows in work right now. Call me some other time." Click.

I'm sure you can now see that conversation going in a whole different direction leading to good results for both.

Equipped and prepared with the skills you've learned in this book, that conversation might go something like this:

"Hi Chris, this is Pat, how are you?"

"Hi Pat, I've been better. I'm putting out a fire here at the office."

"I am so sorry to hear that Chris. What can I do to help?"

A little empathy goes a long way. Simply acknowledging and empathizing shows Chris that Pat cares. And, Pat went beyond just offering sympathy and extended a hand to help.

Ask yourself: Is the goal really to make the sale right then and there? Or, is the ultimate goal to preserve and strengthen the relationship so that many more sales are in Pat's future? We say the sale can wait.

This conversation can now go in a number of directions. Here's one positive way it might go:

"Thanks for offering Chris. I appreciate it. Actually, if you can just give me a half hour to get this done I'll be happy to talk after that."

"Great. I'll give you a call back then Pat. Good luck with the challenge.

Wouldn't you agree you're more likely to get a positive response this way? It's so simple. Your goal is always to preserve and strengthen your business relationships. So remember, whether you're talking to a prospect, a CEO, a co-worker, team member or your boss – *It's Just a Conversation!*

For more information about how you can make the most of every conversation and to download the worksheets from *It's Just a Conversation*, go to
http://ItsJustaConversationBook.com

About the Authors

Trish Carr

is a dynamic international speaker, author, executive business coach and leadership consultant with an expansive background in sales, marketing, customer service and peak performance training. Trish has shared the stage with some of the world's best-known speakers including Jack Canfield, Nancy Matthews, Bob Burg, Loral Langemeier, Steadman Graham and more.

Trish is author of *Sizzling Strategies for Success,* a contributor to the best-selling, *Conversations that Make a Difference,* and to the acclaimed, *Visionaries with Guts.* As a consultant, coach and educator, Trish has worked with leaders and front-line employees in Fortune 500 companies, small and medium-sized businesses, as well as with entrepreneurs and individuals.

As CEO of Revolutionary Consulting, Inc., Trish's passion is to support individuals and business leaders so they reach and exceed their financial goals, optimize their individual and team productivity, and ultimately achieve professional and personal success. Revolutionary Consulting's heart-centered, results-driven coaching, along with solid business strategies ensure that clients get results *now.* To get your free sales building strategy, the *3 P's of Powerful Presentations,* go to http://TrishCarr.com

Trish is co-founder of Women's Prosperity Network, http://WPNGlobal.com, a global enterprise dedicated to inspiring, educating and empowering women and men within a trusted network of professionals. WPN offers online and offline resources, business-building and skill-building tools, and motivation and inspiration for anyone going for more, striving to achieve their goals and live their dreams. Be sure to go to http://WPNGlobal.com/Wow and register for WPN's weekly tele-show, WOW Wednesday, where the WPN community connects to tap into the inspiration, education and motivation that keep you going and growing.

To arrange for Trish to speak at your company or event and to order her books and/or audio programs, please contact:

Trish@TrishCarr.com

(954) 475-2178

http://TrishCarr.com

http://ItsJustaConversationBook.com

Debbie Silverman, president of Consumer Perspective LLC, a market research and strategic planning company, has been conversing with consumers and her clients from Fortune 500 companies to entrepreneurs for over 30 years.

As an accomplished international speaker, author of *7 Secrets to Catapulting Your Business*, and certified NLP (Neuro Linguistic Programming) practitioner, with a degree in psychology, Debbie uses unique strategic engagement techniques to get customers and employees to open up and express what they are really thinking. She shares these strategies in *It's Just a Conversation*.

Debbie has won two Effie Awards for Marketing Excellence, the pre-eminent award in the advertising industry. She has created new businesses, revitalized tired brands, converted prospects into raving fans and most notably, raised the bar on how clients communicate with their customers.

Being a certified NLP practitioner, which is the study of human excellence through our thoughts and words, she has also laid the ground work for a deeper understanding and appreciation of our conversations.

As a two-time top recruiter for a major golf organization (EWGA – Executive Women's Golf Association) and recognized as a Business Woman of the Year nominee, networking and conversing with women and men from all walks of life is what gets Debbie up in the morning. Her passion and motto is KNOW. CONNECT. GROW!

Growing your business is all about having the right conversation with your customers, clients and employees. Learn more about identifying and maximizing ways to delight your customers by going to http://Consumer-Perspective.com now to claim your free e-book, *7 Secrets to Catapulting Your Business.*

For more information about having Debbie speak at your company and to move the conversation forward, please contact:

Debbie@Consumer-Perspective.com
http://Consumer-Perspective.com
http://ItsJustaConversationBook.com
(954) 610-1403

Book Buzz from Amazon:

★★★★★ *"Truly inspirational, engaging, interesting, and practical for any situation and conversation. An essential purchase for every business professional! Simply brilliant!"*
~ Jessica

★★★★★ *"I've barely gotten into the book and already the pages are filled with gems you can begin to use NOW! Silverman and Carr not only offer detailed information on how to say the right words while engaged in business conversations, they laid out the book so you can find that information FAST!"*
~ Peggy Lee Hanson

★★★★★ *"Trish Carr and Debbie Silverman have created the new "must have" book for everyone who wants to succeed in business. This step-by-step guide to communicating in business situations explores both keys to success and pitfalls to avoid, complete with clear real-life examples. This book does an especially fine job in addressing the nonverbal elements of business conversation, which are too frequently ignored or over-simplified... Make this book your new Business Bible -- you can't go wrong with this terrific guide."*
~ Gail Dixon

★★★★★ *"Debbie and Trish have managed to put on paper what a good salesperson has always known. It's Just a Conversation is poignant, intuitive and comprehensive. It's the best guide to sales and other business issues that I've seen in a very long time."*
~ Bruce Borowitz

★★★★★ "I learned something by p.4. I bought this book because Debbie Silverman is a colleague, but I couldn't put it down because the book is terrific. It's well-written, full of insights you can use today, and organized for easy reference. I can't think of anyone who doesn't need it."
~Jann Sabin

★★★★★ "This is an awesome book. As a Toastmaster, I find that many people speaking think that the person/audience understood them. This isn't always the case. These authors have made a significant addition to the Art of Conversation. Finally, a way to say what you mean, mean what you say and be heard and understood! Kudos to the authors! Readers, enjoy and learn!"
~ Adele Alexandre

★★★★★ "Many people fall short of reaching measurable 'Business' success because their communication style and techniques are outdated. 'It's Just a Conversation' will teach you what to say and how to say it in business. You will learn strategies to surge your conversations forward and deliver tangible results for years to come."
~ Sandra Hanesworth

TAKE YOUR CONVERSATIONS TO THE NEXT LEVEL AND GRAB THESE FREE RESOURCES TODAY:

Want a quick reference sheet to make your conversations count? Go to http://ItsJustaConversationBook.com and get *7 Simple Steps to Success in Every Conversation.*

Make your sales presentations pop every time with *The 3 P's of Powerful Presentations*: http://TrishCarr.com

Maximize your relationships with your customers or clients and employees and learn how to delight them. Grab your ebook, *7 Secrets to Catapulting Your Business* at http://Consumer-Perspective.com

Learn how to capitalize on "One Size Does Not Fit All" communication styles to accelerate your sales, your business and your life at http://TrishCarr.com

Online and offline business-building and skill-building tools available at http://WPNGlobal.com

Create more engaging conversations with your customers and employees and grow your bottom line at http://Consumer-Perspective.com

Download the usable worksheets
and access your bonus resources at:
ItsJustaConversationBook.com/downloads

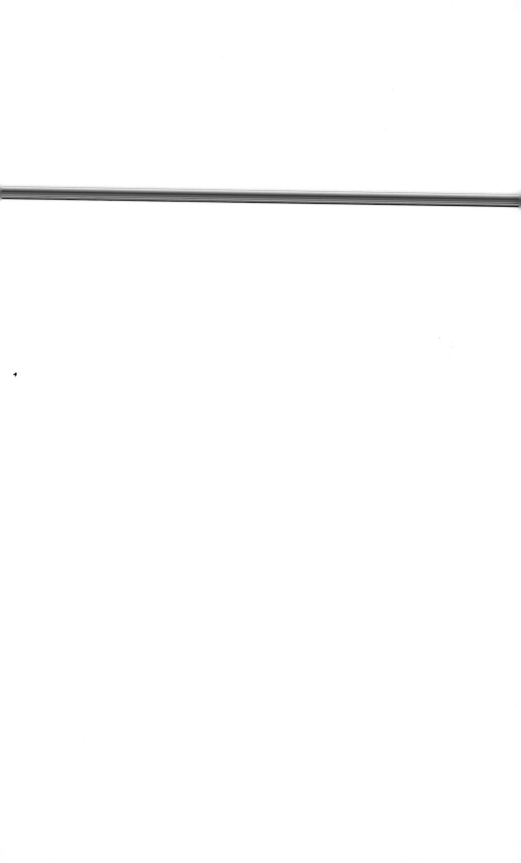